A woman's journey
of spiritual development
in New York

In·sight

MOMENTS OF BEING

Joanna Infeld

Copyright © 2012 by Joanna Infeld

All rights reserved under International Copyright Conventions.
No part of this book may be used or reproduced in any manner
whatsoever without written permission from the publisher.
For further information go to
www.KoraPress.com

Printed in the United States of America

Kora Press is a registered trademark.
ISBN 10: 0-9815509-3-2
ISBN 13: 978-0-9815509-3-0

Book design: Alison Goudreault of iseeideas.com
Interior photos by the author

Kora is a type of pilgrimage and meditation by movement in
the Tibetan Buddhist tradition. A kora is performed by walking
around a mountain, temple, stupa, or other sacred site.

A woman's journey
of spiritual development
in New York

In·sight

MOMENTS OF BEING

Joanna Infeld

From the Publisher

Kora Press is proud to present the third book in a trilogy by Joanna Infeld entitled *In-Sight: Moments of Being*. This trilogy is another in a series of publications dedicated to human development, the search for truth and the human story.

The two earlier parts of the trilogy are titled *In-Formation: Moments of Realization* and *In-Tuition: Moments of Awakening*. Each book is a complete story unto itself and does not need to be read in sequence.

If you enjoy *In-Sight: Moments of Being*, you will probably also enjoy other books by the same author from Kora Press (available online from www.Amazon.com, www.BarnesandNoble.com or www.KoraPress.com):

7 Ages of Woman
Unmasked: Spirit Flares
Dear Gabriel: Letters from a Trainee Angel
God's Spies: Gratefully Aging
A Garden of Qualities: Living a Quality Life

The Publisher wishes to give special thanks to Alison Goudreault for her inspiration and contribution to the design of this book.

From the Publisher page 5
Foreword page 9

One	The Move	page 11
Two	Building Character	page 17
Three	The River That Flows Both Ways	page 21
Four	Generosity	page 29
Five	Joan of Arc	page 37
Six	Compassion	page 49
Seven	Cleopatra's Needle	page 59
Eight	Value	page 67
Nine	The News Building	page 75
Ten	Justice	page 83
Eleven	Alice in Wonderland	page 87
Twelve	Belief	page 93
Thirteen	The Cloisters	page 97
Fourteen	Humility	page 103
Fifteen	The Garden of Stones	page 109
Sixteen	Service	page 115
Seventeen	Grand Central Terminal	page 121
Eighteen	Wonder	page 131
Nineteen	The MET	page 139
Twenty	Persistence	page 153
Twenty-One	The Rubin Museum	page 161
Twenty-Two	Honor	page 175
Twenty-Three	Imagine	page 179
Twenty-Four	Love	page 183
Twenty-Five	Love, New York	page 189
Twenty-Six	Trust	page 193

In-Tuition; Moments of Awakening:
Chapter One The Discovery page 199

In-Sight; Moments of Being tells the story of one woman's spiritual journey at the third of three progressive levels of understanding. It is more a parable than a factual relating of events, though the background to this spiritual journey is very real—the story takes place in the city of New York and at some of its many sites which hold a deeper esoteric meaning.

This is the story of the main character's inner journey and development, as she questions her purpose and mission in life and decides to undertake a search for knowledge and the truth. Although external events take place, what is more important is the growth of awareness and the development of consciousness of the young woman, Barbara Faye. To her surprise, she discovers that a real journey into the mystery of life will always produce a further hunger to find out more. This is the transformational journey from being a student of a mysterious Master, whom she visits on the astral plane during the hours of the night, to becoming a healer and a teacher herself.

I wish to thank David Price Francis, my husband and partner, for his ideas and advice in writing this book.

Joanna Infeld

Chapter One

The Move

It was a split moment's decision. My marriage was finished and I had lost my job. Just when I began feeling sorry for myself, my old friend Bobbie called me, out of the blue. "Come to New York," she said. "I am house sitting for this writer I am working for and I'm all on my own in this apartment with a cat and a dog. He's gone for a month, doing a tour promoting his latest book. So come and keep me company."

That was it. I decided to pack my bags and move on. It was time to stop feeling sorry for myself and to give myself a chance at a fresh start. I managed to find a cheap flight and flew to La Guardia airport. Bobbie was there and helped guide me to the car she was driving. I was surprised it was a Mercedes.

"You are doing well for yourself," I said.

"It's not mine," she pointed out. "It's his."

"So what do you do for this writer of yours? "I asked as soon as we left the parking lot and started driving up the Grand Central Parkway toward Manhattan.

"I'm his secretary, his editor, his typist, his dog walker and his shopper," she said. She caught my eye as I looked at her inquisitively. "One thing I am not," she said, "is his girlfriend or his lover. He's too old for me and, anyway, he has this long-term relationship with his agent."

"But they don't live together? " I asked.

In·sight: MOMENTS OF BEING

"No, they don't," she said.

We crossed into Manhattan. It was my first visit to New York. Although I had seen the city many times, both in movies and on pictures, the scale of the traffic, the buildings and the energy was quite overwhelming. I could feel the intensity radiating from the ground—it was palpable all around as we drove through the streets of the Upper East Side. I couldn't put my finger on it, but I could feel the invigorating effect watching the traffic and the people was having on me.

The way I had lost my job was sudden and unexpected. I had been working as a dispatcher for a furniture company and I was responsible for delivering orders to one of the five areas of the city. I thought the company was doing well and that I was performing my duties conscientiously, punctually and with good attention to detail. So nothing had prepared me for the shock of suddenly being dismissed. That Monday I saw some new faces around the office and I was told by one of my co-workers that these people—two men and a woman—had been called in to reorganize the company and to help downsize the operation. They were from a company called CGC. When I asked what the name meant or referred to, I was told that CGC stood for Corporate Growth Consultants and that it was a company that specialized in reorganizing and restructuring companies that were not performing well. The three employees of CGC occupied three small offices and they were clearly interviewing various people, as we could observe different employees entering their offices, then coming out again, packing their belongings and quickly leaving the building. The atmosphere was tense and I could feel the mounting pressure as the day wore on.

Then came my turn. I was asked into one of the offices and I was invited to sit in a chair in front of a large desk. Behind the desk sat a young man in a dark suit and white shirt. I was fascinated by his tie—it had a blue background with an abstract yellow leaf pattern.

"We have been asked to reorganize the company so it can become profitable again," he said.

The Move

"So I heard," I said, wondering what was coming next.

"We have decided to consolidate the delivery routes," he continued. "There is not enough business to warrant five routes." There was a moment of silence and then, at last, he explained what this meant to me. "We are eliminating two routes," he said, "which includes yours. Your route will be divided up among the remaining three dispatchers." Another moment of silence while I was taking this all in.

"In simple terms, that means we are letting you go," he said. "The employees who are staying are those who have been here the longest. You have only been here for"—he looked at his notes—"14 months. You will receive two weeks' salary and you will leave immediately."

I sat there incredulously. I couldn't believe this was really happening. All I could think of was how could anyone take over my files, my systems and my neatly planned schedules.

"What about my computer password?" I asked.

"Don't worry about that," he said. "Just take your things and go home." There was no sympathy or apology in his voice. I sat there, stunned, unable to move.

"You will cry," he said unexpectedly. "Once you get home and realize what has happened, you will be upset. It's only natural," he added with a smile that felt as cold as ice. I got up. He stood up as well and handed me an envelope.

"Here is your check," he said, "and here is my card." He took a business card out of his pocket. "Call me if you need counseling or help in finding a new job," he said.

I took both items and walked out of the office. I went to my desk and started gathering my belongings. Strangely enough, it felt like a relief to be leaving and there was no sorrow in me about it.

On my way home I started to feel upset. I felt like a loser—I had lost a job which I believed was going well. As I held onto my plastic bag with my diary, my pictures and my lunch box, I realized what was happening in the energy realms around me. There is a record within the energy field of human civilizations that has written within it the experiences of all the people who had ever been fired or lost their jobs for whatever reason. The insecurity, the fear, the uncertainty and the upset were all just waiting to pounce on me and claim me as one of their own. Thankfully I was sensitive enough to recognize that these feelings were nothing to do with me and I realized at that moment that I wanted to defy them and not become their next victim. What a difference that realization had made! It was like backing off a pack of wolves or a dark cloud that was ready to descend and engulf me into its inky blackness.

I now realize how powerful a feeling can be, once it has developed and established a history of being contributed to by many people over several generations. For example, even though I am not a Jew, I can feel the reverence of Jews going to *shul* on a Saturday morning. The dedication and religious devotion of all the Jews throughout the centuries and all over the world has built a powerful momentum within the energy realms, to which even non-Jews can effectively respond if they choose to do so. Once I realized that every Saturday I was picking up these feelings, I began to consciously incorporate what I was feeling into my day. And so the tradition of a "Saturday grateful morning contemplation" began—a time to think about all the people and things I was grateful for.

At the opposite end of the spectrum, I would feel a mounting depression on Sunday night when millions of people would be projecting to their Monday morning back-to-work mode, after a weekend of enjoying their freedom. I realized that this was nothing to do with me and I learned that I have to struggle to fend off this specter of despondency. So Sunday night became my "ode to joy," a time when I deliberately thought about all the activities that brought me joy and all the moments when I had felt happy. I eventually learned to prepare meditations for both these occasions. This practice made me feel that I was at least trying to make a difference in the unseen worlds of human emotions, which I came to view as a vast lake or sea, within which all of people's feelings—both past and present—would be swirling together—indestructible and present all the time. This collective

The Move

power is ready to respond to a frequency that is similar to it and to add to any one person's experience, providing their emotions are strong enough to make an impression in the energy field of the planet.

I could see why depression would cause more depression as it would summon a similar response from the pool of emotions; likewise, joy would call for joy and gratitude for more gratitude. I also learned that I could deliberately seek out a feeling or an emotion, even if I did not, or was not able to, feel it at a depth that would automatically cause a response. So, for example, if I needed courage, I learned to act courageously, according to what I had observed in the behavior of other people who were more courageous then I—known either from movies, literature or from personal experience—and sometimes courage would come in response

I once went to a workshop where they were teaching about healing with the hands. It was a large conference room in a hotel, full of people. When they asked for volunteers, I put my hand up and was asked to come up onto the stage. I was shaking with nerves but somehow managed to get up there and followed the instructions of the presenter. Holding out my hands I was making sweeping movements inside the energy field above a man who was lying on the healing table on the stage. I could feel the energy coming out of my hands and I knew that he was feeling it too. "It was very relaxing," he said later, "and I almost fell asleep."

Other people later came up to me and remarked how courageous I had been to volunteer with a room full of people. I knew this was how they saw me but I also realized that because I had put my hand up, even before I had realized I had done so, courage had responded to that act and that although I had not felt courageous at all, other people recognized that I was a brave person. For the rest of the time I was at that three-day workshop, people treated me with great respect, often turning toward me and asking me what I thought of this idea or that concept.

These experiences and realizations helped me on the day I was fired. Understanding that the depression that seemed to be hovering around me (I could feel it just above my head) was not my own, helped me negate it and push it aside. I was convinced that I had lost my job because better experiences lay ahead of me. So instead of giving into despair, I decided to celebrate. I phoned a friend and we both went out to dinner that night. We spent the evening making plans and fantasizing about what we would do if only we had the money to do it with.

We arrived at Bobbie's temporary home on Second Avenue. We walked upstairs pulling my suitcase behind us—the apartment was on the fourth floor of a walk-up.

"Not the most salubrious abode," said Bobbie as she opened the door with a key. Bobbie always had a way with words and favored five syllable words where she could have expressed herself with two.

The apartment was indeed small, but it was tidy and clean. There were three bedrooms—the smaller one was used as an office and had a desk with an Apple computer on it. Next to the computer was a stack of papers, neatly piled. Clearly it was the writer's new manuscript, printed on the laser printer that was sitting on a table next to the desk. It looked like the manuscript was ready for revision or for submission to a publisher. There was also a narrow bed which was to become my sleeping place for the next week.

"You can hang up your clothes in the closet in the large bedroom," Bobbie said. "The bathroom is at the other end of the apartment, next to the kitchen. Here are a couple of towels." She placed the towels on the bed. "A cleaning lady comes in every two weeks on a Thursday, so make sure you tidy up by Wednesday night. She doesn't speak English, but she does understand a few basic words." I always found it strange how people clean up their homes before the cleaning person arrives. We do half their work for them. Perhaps hiring a cleaning lady is just an incentive to keep things tidy and clean.

Chapter Two

Building Character

That night I dreamed I was at a mysterious school where a wise master was teaching a group of students about the secrets of the universe. I was attending a lecture in a large hall and listening attentively as this learned sage was explaining how everything in this world consists of energy and how even material objects, fauna and flora as well as humans are all made of condensed and slowed down energy. In my dream I was fascinated by this concept and at the end of the lecture I went up to the Master to tell him how much I had enjoyed his lecture. As I walked up to him, both he and our surroundings began to look vaguely familiar. I felt I had been here before. In fact, I was certain I had.

"It is good to see you again," he said and and I was not in the least bit surprised that he did.

"It is good to be back," I replied.

"Now that you have returned to study at the next level," he said, "I have a new program for you." He paused as I eagerly awaited to hear what he had in mind.

"I will give you tasks to fulfill and the purpose of these tasks is for you to collect qualities, like care, compassion, patience, humility and generosity. These qualities will help strengthen your character and build charisma, which you will need to fulfill your duties that lie ahead. Every night there will be a new lesson and each lesson will involve learning about a specific quality, which you will then be able to add to your strengths and use whenever needed. You need to acquire these and many other such traits, but in a safe way. I will guide you on this journey so that you will eventually be able to teach and help others."

I must have looked surprised because he soon added:

"There is much for you to do in this life. Like everyone alive on Earth at this time, you have a mission to find and fulfill. But unlike most people, you were given special talents and abilities, and it is for you to use these wisely."

"What gifts?" I asked, incredulously.

"You already know that you can heal," he said. "You are also clairvoyant and telepathic. You sometimes see the future and sometimes you can connect to the past. These are great gifts. Use them wisely to help and teach others. The world badly needs people who can heal. Many people all over the world are nursing wounds and scars that are not just physical, but mental, emotional and psychological as well. You are able to heal all these hurts, but be careful to always heal yourself first. You are your most important patient and without health you are of no use to anyone else."

A group of students had gathered around as we stood in the middle of the great hall. They were all listening intently, hanging onto his words.

"The next stage will be both enjoyable and difficult. Each test will be devised to target a specific quality. You will be receiving instruction during the hours of the night and when you wake up in the morning, you will think it was all just a dream. But it will be more than a phantom or a fantasy because in your astral form—that is your energy body—you will revisit this center and learn about one aspect that you need to bring into yourself to be more effective as a teacher and a healer. Are you ready to commit to my discipline and my requirements?"

"I am," I replied, though a million questions seemed to be running around in my head: questions like, will I remember what I learn, and, what kind of teacher am I to become? Who and where are the students? How can I find them? As if reading my thoughts, the Master added, "The students will find you when the time is right. You will know what to do. The sessions at this school will prepare you for your destiny which will unfold before you. Listen to your instinct and you will know when the time is right.

"The energy of your planet is changing daily and in the Age of Aquarius it is becoming more and more charged. Many more people will start seeing auras and the energy around plants and animals; more people will discover that, like you, they can heal with their hands. Others will start receiving messages about the future and will be able to hear other people's thoughts and feelings. All of this might appear scary at the beginning, and people will need an education about how to live with and develop their gifts. This is where you come in—you will be able to reassure them that clairvoyance and telepathy are natural skills, known from ancient times, and that when put to good use these abilities can in turn serve others and help them understand the energies around them as well as planetary and cosmic change."

I felt overwhelmed. I had to think about all this, but something inside me knew that he was right and that I was born onto this planet with a purpose and a mission. I just needed to embrace my destiny and make it my own. I wondered what it was that was instructing me and showing me glimpses of my future. Again, as if reading my thoughts, the Master explained, "It's your intuition," he said.

> *Finch! Rise up and play*
> *Those liquid notes that steal men's hearts away!*
>
> The Conference of the Birds
> Farid ud-Din Attar

Chapter Three

The River That Flows Both Ways

The first day after I had arrived Bobbie took me around the neighborhood and showed me where the shops were, which were her favorite restaurants and the bar Elaine where celebrities liked to hang out. Apparently Woody Allen could still be seen there on occasion playing the trumpet on a Monday night.

Despite the excitement and the distractions, I felt I had come to New York for a reason. It wasn't about the celebrities or the variety of food, and it wasn't even about finding a lucrative job. Although I needed to earn money to pay for my meals and board, there was something much more personal that I felt was influencing my decision. Still very much under the influence of my previous night's dream, I thought it was about building character and helping others do the same.

We were sitting at the kitchen table having breakfast—New York bagels from Eli's foodstore and bakery—when Bobbie's cell phone rang. As she answered it, she whispered, "That's him," and got up to walk into the bedroom where she could speak in privacy.

I waited for a few minutes, sipping my tea, and soon she was back. "He's coming back tomorrow," she announced. "The last leg of his tour was cancelled because the bookstore where he was going to have a book signing has been repossessed by the bank." I looked concerned, so she quickly added, "He knows you are here and he says you can stay one more night if you sleep on the sofa in the living room. That way it will give you time to find a place to stay."

I felt somewhat relieved, but still worried, because I did not know how to start looking.

"Well, go onto Craigs list," Bobbie said as she took a final bite of her bagel, having sat back down at the table. "You can find anything there. That's how I found this job. Perhaps you can find something like this, too."

"I'm no editor, Bobbie. You know that. And I don't have five years of experience teaching English. But maybe I can find something a little more suitable."

A moment later we were sitting at the computer. We soon found some jobs that seemed possible—top of the list was a receptionist and administrative assistant for a health food company. The Healthy Gourmet was located nearby and it looked like I had the necessary qualifications, having worked as an administrative assistant and dispatcher for a furniture company. I felt more positive already. I applied for a few other jobs on line as well and very soon I had a response—within the hour I had three appointments that were scheduled to take place over the next few days.

Looking for apartments on line was much more difficult. Rents were expensive and I couldn't find anything within my price range. We walked around and visited local apartment buildings. There were several places where apartments were available but, again, nothing within the range which I could afford. It seemed like I would need to move out to Queens or the Bronx.

Later that afternoon Bobbie and I were sitting at the kitchen table, exhausted, sipping a cup of coffee when suddenly we heard a key in the lock opening the door.

"Oh my God," Bobbie exclaimed, "he's home early." Sure enough, in walked a middle-aged man with a suitcase in tow and a raincoat over his arm. He had a short greying beard, long hair down to his shoulders and glasses.

"I didn't expect you until tomorrow," Bobbie said, suddenly flustered. She got up from the table and was reaching out to help the man pull his suitcase over the threshold.

"This is my friend Barbara," she said. The man stood in front of the open door and said, "I'm Mark. Bobbie probably told you about me. I live here."

I got up from the table, unsure what to do next. "Yes," I said, "I know. I'll pack my bag."

"I got an earlier flight," Mark said as he closed the door behind him. "It's all right. You can stay a couple of nights until you find somewhere to live. Just clear your things out of my office."

"I'll do that straight away," I said.

"Come on Barbs, I'll help you change the sheets," Bobbie added. We both went into the office and started stripping the bed. Bobbie brought out some fresh linen from the closet and soon the bed was ready and I had packed my personal belongings and wheeled my suitcase into the living room.

By next morning I was glad to have the three interviews lined up over the next few days, but worried that I still had nowhere to live. We were sitting at the kitchen table having breakfast together. Bobbie had made an omelette and although the little kitchen felt a bit crowded, the atmosphere was surprisingly relaxed. Mark was regaling us with anecdotes from his book signing tour. I think he was glad to have a receptive audience. He had brought back with him copies of his latest book. Titled *The Strangest Quest* it was about a young man's spiritual journey which took him to many countries in the world. There were stories in the book about time spent with magicians, shamans, gurus, wizards, kahunas, elders and sages from all kinds of esoteric traditions. It appeared that Mark had visited all five continents in search of a story and that many of the incidents described in the book had actually happened to him.

"But best of all are the adventures that take place right here in New York," Mark said as he cut into his omelette. "Today, if you girls have nothing better to do, I'll take you on a tour of one of my favorite spots." We both looked at him wide-eyed. We then quickly glanced at each other and replied in unison.

"Yes, please," I said, delighted.

"Where are we going?" asked Bobbie.

We took the subway to 14th Street. From there we walked to the High Line Elevated Park—created on a disused elevated railway on the west side of Midtown Manhattan.

"Most people who visit the Elevated Park—and millions do every year—miss this particular piece of art. Maybe it is unremarkable when simply viewed as colored panes of glass in a series of windows. But when you read about its history, you can appreciate the thought and care that has gone into this unique design," explained Mark.

Between 15th and 16th Streets on the elevated park is the artistic display titled *The River That Flows Both Ways* by Spencer Finch. The 700 laminated glass panels with color film inter-layer are easy to miss if one is not aware they are there. The artwork is reminiscent of medieval stain glass windows. They form a remarkable piece of art with an intriguing history behind it. There was a plaque in front of the windows designed by Finch and we read about the history of his artwork. It explained that *The River That Flows Both Ways* was inspired by the Hudson River. The window panes document a 700 minute—11 hours, 40 minutes—journey on the river in a single day. The title is a translation of *Muhheakantuck*—the Native American name for the Hudson. It refers to the river's natural flow in two directions, just like the trains that used to travel both ways on the High Line.

The Hudson was and still is an active route for the transportation of goods into Manhattan. The river and the High Line have always been linked to their geography, their function and their imprint on the industrial legacy of the city.

On June 12th, 2008 from a tugboat drifting on Manhattan's West Side and past the High Line, Finch photographed the river's surface once every minute. The color of each panel of glass was based on a single pixel point in each photograph and arranged chronologically within the High Line tunnel's existing steel mullions.

Time is translated into a grid reading from left to right and top to bottom, capturing the very reflective and translucent conditions of the water's surface. The work, like the river, is experienced differently each time, depending on the light level and the atmospheric conditions of the site. In the narrative orientation, the glass reveals Finch's impossible quest for the color of water.

Finch's artwork brings together technologies that are both ancient (colored panes of glass) and modern (concentrating on a single pixel on a computer screen). He has managed to freeze his impressions, captured during his journey along the river. Thus he has conveyed to the spectator his attempt at the impossible—to capture a moment of reflection, light and hue—and preserve it for posterity.

Born in 1962 in New Haven, Connecticut, Spencer Finch was known to have worked in a number of artistic media, including paint, photography, glass and with filters. He was especially concerned with capturing moments by trying to reproduce the light and color of a specific place and time. He has attempted to reproduce by artificial means the light of the full moon, the setting sun, the night sky or the color of a waterfall covered in mist.

Finch would record the invisible and the non-physical world. He applied a scientific method to do so, using a colorimeter that reads the average temperature and color of light. He then translated what he recorded relying on his own power of observation, his sensitivity and his poetic interpretation.

I felt that Finch's work added a sense of wonder to the High Line as one could visibly compare the view of the Hudson River with the artist's

In·sight: MOMENTS OF BEING

impression of a brief moment in time.

Energetically every object or living being contains its history as well as its present—where it came from, the originating spark and the story of its unfolding. An oak tree contains the history of being an acorn, just as we humans can tap into memories from childhood and even from the womb of our mother.

Knowing the story behind an event or a design can increase the viewer's value for what they see, providing insight to the inspiration and origins of what has caused it to be conceived in the first place.

A series of 21 windows might not look like very much but once a person delves into the story behind their design, one can better appreciate the care and time taken to choose the right colors to portray the mood and beauty of a river at a very specific and unique moment in time.

To choose one pixel out of one photograph and then to translate that into a colored glass pane, Finch must have examined and considered thousands of pixels before choosing the precise one which ended up as part of his unique design.

The windows do not tell the whole story of the river that flows both ways, but rather it freezes a unique moment in time on a particular day and then from that original photograph one tiny fragment is selected and translated into colored glass. It's a bit like a photograph album from a wedding, where there are close up portraits of some of the people, perhaps a picture of the rings, the cake or the flowers and several group photographs. In no way does such an album relate the whole story and give justice to the emotions of the people involved, the many words spoken or the promises made. But it is never meant to tell the whole story—just a few chosen details and impressions, capturing a moment, a look, a smile and a feeling.

For the Hudson river these moments are translated into color—a shimmering reflection of the setting sun or a cloud or the image of a building reflected from the water in hues of grays and blues.

Our lives are like that as we combine our momentous moments and memories like pearls on a string, never really capturing a view of the totality of a journey until perhaps at the very end, when we can see it all and marvel at the multiplicity of our endeavors to lead a meaningful existence. Moments is what we have—one pixel of an entire picture, one unique glimpse of reality, as we view it through the lens of our experiences, biases, upbringing and education.

We are forever piecing these moments together to discover the truth of our lives. Who are we? Like the panes in the windows created by Finch—how can we know what all our moments will amount to until our efforts are completed?

A river that flows both ways traces two very different paths—coming and going.

"The river that flows both ways is like the energy flow within a person's aura," said Mark. "We are always taking in and giving out energy. The quality of what we pass on to others depends on what we allow ourselves to take in. That's why it is so important to build filters and standards so that we can control what comes into our field and what goes out toward another person. It's like having a system of dikes and sluices to build one's character and become the person we would want to be."

We were sitting on the wooden benches overlooking Tenth Avenue. The benches are built on a bridge above the street and are constructed on steps descending toward a large picture window. It felt a bit like we were suspended in space, looking down at the traffic flowing below us. Just like the river Hudson, the traffic was flowing both ways. I felt that this day was like a continuation of my dreamscape and that Mark's interpretation of the energy traffic was an invitation to take control of my life and to decide who and what I wanted to become.

Chapter Four

Generosity

That night, as soon as I fell asleep I dreamed I was back at the mystery school.

It was morning and I was summoned to see the Master after breakfast. As soon as I entered his study, he stood up and handed me a $100 dollar bill.

"I want you to take this," he said "and go into town for two hours and spend it. Gregory the driver will take you there."

I looked at the bill in his hand and hesitated for a moment, wondering what lesson was he concocting for me today. He noticed my hesitation and said, "You won't be able to work it out. I don't know myself what will come of it. All I know is that there is learning in everything. Therefore, whatever happens today with you and this little bit of green paper, as well as what does not happen, there will be a lesson to help you in your development."

I smiled and took the banknote. Whatever else might happen today, this was going to be an enjoyable lesson as well as an education. I decided to not think about my training but to have a break and follow my feelings rather than my mind. I put the note in my pocket and said, "Thank you," as I proceeded to leave the room.

As I left the building I could see the car was already waiting and Gregory the driver was standing beside the door. He saw me approach and opened the back door of the car. I got in and we were soon on our way, heading into town. For the first few minutes of the short drive we were both silent, but then Gregory began a conversation by saying, "I was told that I should take you into town. Do you know what you will be doing there?" he asked.

"I am supposed to spend a hundred dollars," I replied. Can you take me to the shops?"

"I was told that I should drop you off on the main square and pick you up two hours later. There are plenty of shops all around there. Some nice ones, too. I'm sure you will have a good time."

"I'm looking forward to it."

There the conversation ended. Funny, how banal and normal it all seemed on the surface, and yet I felt something else going on underneath the polite exchange. I felt he knew about the test, but acted as if it was an ordinary outing on an ordinary day.

We entered the town and soon arrived at the central square. In the middle of the square there was a large lawn with trees and a pond with a fountain in the middle. The four streets surrounding the square were full of cafés, restaurants and all kinds of shops, selling almost anything one could ever desire—clothes, kitchen utensils, arts and crafts, books, carpets, sportswear, shoes, gadgets, trinkets, furniture, appliances, frames, glass, crystal, jewelry and more and more... On one side of the square there was a large stone church that looked very old. It had a grand set of steps leading up to the front portal.

Gregory parked the car alongside the central park and got out to open the door for me.

"I'll be back here in two hours," he said as I got out. He then got back in the car and drove away. I stood there for a moment, wondering what to do next, suddenly feeling rather alone and very unsure of myself. I had a hundred dollars in my pocket—I could buy a single item, like a ring or a pair of earrings and spend the entire amount in five minutes, or I could linger and look around for a while. I could also take advantage of the fine weather and sit down in one of the open air pavement cafés that seemed to be very busy at this time. The place was bustling with people—shoppers, passers by, window shoppers, mothers with baby carriages, school children going home for lunch...

I slowly crossed the road and looked into the first window of the first shop I could see. There was a display of clothes and right in front of my very eyes there was a silk green dress on a mannequin, with a price tag on it—$99.99. I knew straight away that it would look great on me and that under any other circumstance I would be interested in trying it on. But today I could only think that spending the money given to me in this way would be folly. After all, this was a test and a learning. I felt that it did not fit to be so personal about it and somehow the importance of attractive clothes seemed to recede away from my mind into the distance. I smiled to myself as I noted these feelings and I slowly walked away.

I looked around and my attention was drawn to the church. I felt that it would be a good idea to retreat from the busy crowds and cool off inside, while contemplating my today's predicament. So I crossed the street back onto the square and walked through the park toward the imposing building. It was pleasant and calming to walk among the trees and as I passed by the fountain, I could feel the cool freshness of the water; the sound of the constant flow also seemed reassuring with its constant rhythm.

I crossed the street again and stood at the bottom of the church steps and looked up. It was an imposing edifice, built to resemble a medieval cathedral, rather than a church. The spire towered over the town like a sentinel and the huge stone portal disallowed casual entrance; it caused me to stop and think for a moment about my reasons for entering. It felt almost as if something or someone was asking the questions—why was I there, and what did I want.

On entering the church I could feel an immediate drop in temperature. It was simply constructed with huge pillars on either side and a large nave leading to an altar at the front. Not ornate, but there were paintings and statues along either side of the nave.

There was hardly anyone there and I slipped into one of the back pews to gather my thoughts and contemplate my next move. I could feel the pressure of the outside dropping away from me, and everything began to seem quite distant, even the school and the Master and the teachings. In fact, I felt closer to something subliminal and unseen than I had ever felt before in my life. I don't know how long I sat there, but after a while I began to feel the chill and decided to move toward the door. The moment I got up I remembered my task and the banknote, still lodged in the pocket of my jeans.

As I walked out of the church into the sunlight, I noticed a beggar, leaning on two crutches. He had placed his hat in front of him on the ground with a few coins inside it. He was standing on one leg with the other one clearly amputated at the knee and his trouser leg pinned up behind him. I looked at him and he noticed me, so he stretched out his hand, as he mumbled something, like, "Help a poor veteran, give generously to those who are less fortunate than you…"

I stopped. I was utterly convinced that this was part of the test and that the requirement was upon me to respond. At once I felt relief that now I could get rid of the note in my pocket and complete the task. I reached for the $100 bill and, after a short moment of hesitation, as I briefly scanned mentally all the possible things I could have done with it, I dropped the note into his hat. He probably couldn't see how much it was, but just the sight of the paper caused his face to brighten as he exclaimed in delight, "Thank you, thank you, lady. May God bless you."

I turned away and ran down the stairs. Then, across the street and into the park and back by the fountain to where Gregory had originally parked the car. He wasn't there yet, so I sat down on a nearby bench and waited while a couple of children played on the path in front of me, throwing and catching a ball.

I didn't have to wait long. The car soon pulled up and in a few moments we were on our way. Gregory started up a brief conversation:

"How did it go?" he asked.

"Very well," I replied, feeling satisfied with myself for not having spent the money on myself. I felt this was the purpose of the exercise and that I had done the correct thing; but I wasn't going to tell him. He nevertheless wanted to know.

"So, what did you do?" he asked. "I don't see any packages," he added.

"Oh, not very much. I looked around and then I went to church."

"That sounds interesting. What did you find there?"

"Not much," I replied, attempting to end the conversation. But then I felt I was being rude, so I added: "A little bit of peace on a busy day."

Gregory looked at me in the rear view mirror.

"Ah, that's nice," he said. And that was really the end of the conversation.

Back at the school, I went straight to the interview room and knocked on the door. Somehow I knew the Master would be there waiting for me. Sure enough, the reply came almost immediately, "Come in." He was sitting at a small round table writing and as I entered he looked up from his notes and pointed to the seat at the other side of the table. "Sit down," he said, and as I did as he requested, he asked, "What happened?"

I proceeded to tell him the story of the past hours I had spent in town with as much detail as I could remember; I did not want to assume that I knew what was important and thus leave out some detail that might appear significant to him. I also tried to be as honest as I could, although my self-satisfaction must have manifested through the words, especially when I came to the episode with the beggar. He listened attentively and when I was quite finished, he paused for a moment, and then proceeded with his commentary.

"What a great lesson you have learned today!" he said. "This was a hundred dollars well spent indeed. The lesson has clearly been about generosity. If you look at the root of the word, it is close to the word *generate*. Generosity is something we generate in self, but the power and quality of it will depend on the reason why we do it. In your case the quality of your generosity was rather poor. You did not give out of care for the misfortune of another or because you wanted to see poverty eliminated from the world.

You gave to fulfill your tasking and therefore you gave selfishly. It might have been less selfish to have bought that dress—at least you would have followed your natural inclination and been more true to yourself. However, you did brighten another man's day and that is always a good thing to do. But that is not real generosity, for real generosity is giving of oneself, not just giving money or things. Real generosity is backed up with sentiment and genuine care. As in the parable of the widow's mite, it is not the amount that one gives that counts, but the amount which one has left over.

"So, what you need to do now is to rethink your motive and at least rewrite it to yourself. Ask yourself whether you want to be generous as a way of life and if so, make sure that your actions and your motives match your intentions."

He paused for a moment. I felt chastised, but I had to agree with him. I nodded and replied, "I will." The voice came out rather timidly, which surprised me, but I could understand why.

"Good," he said. "You have a lot of work to do. Come back when you are ready." He smiled at me quite disarmingly and turned his gaze toward his notes.

"Thank you," I said as I got up and quietly left the room, closing the door behind me.

*Now the flames they followed Joan of Arc
as she came riding through the dark.*

Leonard Cohen

Chapter Five

Joan of Arc

Sleeping on a stranger's couch at the age of 32 was an interesting experience. I felt somewhat insecure about what could happen next, but also incredibly free. I sat up in bed in the middle of the night and burst out laughing—I had very little money, I was in a new city where I hardly knew anyone, I had no job and so far no real prospects either. And yet, facing the unknown felt like totally the right place to be. It was like a tonic—new, exciting and different, as though I was given a new lease of life. As long as I held onto the sense of adventure and freedom, everything felt possible. But the moment I slipped into worry and insecurity, the future looked bleak and menacing. It was at that moment that I really felt the power of the mind. I believed that I did indeed hold the keys to my own future and that I could shape it any way I wanted to. The decision was mine and mine alone.

I got up and went to the kitchen to fetch a glass of water. To my surprise Mark was up and sitting at the breakfast table with some papers and a cup of coffee in front of him.

"I work best at night," he explained as he looked up and saw me standing in the doorway, obviously surprised.

I picked up a glass from the dishwasher and poured myself a glass of water.

In·sight: MOMENTS OF BEING

"Do you mind if I sit here for a moment?" He gestured toward the chair opposite and I sat down.

"What are you writing about?" I asked.

"It's the story of a wizard. A modern day wizard."

"Do you mean like Harry Potter?"

"No, more like Merlin. Did you know that a merlin is a bird?"

"Yes, but what has that got to do with being a wizard?"

"Merlin was a station or a level of attainment for wizards and students of the occult. In ancient Persia they had a conference of birds—they used the word bird to describe a human who had the ability to fly in the energy realms. There are many kinds of energy travel. There's astral travel, mental travel, emotional travel, soul travel and spirit travel. A merlin could mentally travel, whereas an eagle was adept at soul travel."

"How fascinating," I said, genuinely interested. "I never heard of that."

"Well, not surprising," Mark said. "The Conference of Birds was a secret society. One was only allowed in with a certain level of development."

"What did one need to do to get in?" I asked.

"Nothing physically," Mark replied. "But one needed to be clairvoyant enough to answer the admitting examiner's questions without speaking."

"What do you mean, without speaking?" I asked.

"Telepathically," he replied. "The examiner would mentally transmit the question and the student would reply in their mind, projecting an image into their energy field which the examiner would in turn pick up and then decide whether it was accurate or not."

"I had no idea that was possible."

"Oh yes, telepathy is a real skill. Let's try it. Concentrate for a moment and see if you can pick up an image. I will transmit a basic symbol to you." As soon as he said that, I could see a blue triangle in my mind, almost as clearly as if I were seeing it drawn on a piece of paper.

"A triangle," I said.

"That's right." Mark smiled. "It's not one of the five basic images used to test a person's clairvoyant abilities. The five they use in testing are a circle, wavy lines, a rectangle, a five-pointed star and a cross. A triangle is easy to pick up," he added a moment later. "You are obviously psychic."

"I am? No one has ever said that to me before. But I have had many experiences in my life when I was able to pick up something specific about a person's past or even about the future, like when I predicted that a jewelry store I had walked into would be robbed. No one listened to me but the very next day thieves broke into the store and made away with thousands of dollars' worth of merchandise."

"Okay, let's try something else. Tell me where I was born."

"I have no idea," I quickly replied, but soon a picture started forming up in my head. "I am seeing a darkened room with large windows looking out onto a garden. I don't know where this is, but I can see a calendar on the wall. The writing looks like Russian. The year is 1967."

"That's absolutely correct," Mark said. "I was born in the Ukraine which was part of Russia then, so the calendar would have probably been in Russian."

"I wouldn't know the difference between Russian and Ukrainian," I said. "That's amazing. I didn't know I could do that."

"It helped that I was thinking of my grandparents' home," Mark said. "We left the Ukraine when I was a baby, but I have been back since then and I know what the room where I was born looks like."

Suddenly I felt really tired. "I'm going back to bed," I said.

"Being telepathic is tiring," Mark explained. "You are tapping into the energetic field of another person. It drains your energies. So don't do it too often."

"I won't," I said as a yawn escaped me. "Good night."

"Good night," Mark said.

The next morning Bobbie had some errands to run and I had a job interview later that afternoon, so I decided to accompany her to get out of Mark's way. I still felt tired after the previous night but I was also keen to explore more areas of the city. That was when something quite miraculous happened. Or maybe it was just a coincidence, but to me it felt like a miracle. On our way downstairs we saw an older lady who was coming upstairs with two shopping bags.

"Good morning Mrs. Green," Bobbie said from a few stairs above the second floor landing. Mrs. Green had just pulled her keys out of her pocket and was about to open the door to her apartment when she looked up and saw Bobbie and I walking downstairs.

"Hello Bobbie," she said. "Bobbie, can I ask you something?"

"Certainly, Mrs. Green. What is it?"

"Well, I need to go away to see my daughter. I promised I would help her look after her two children while she goes away on a business trip. I'll be away for a month and I don't know what to do about my two cats, Moggie and Duchess. Do you know of anyone who could housesit for me for a month?"

We were now on the landing, standing beside Mrs. Green. I could not believe the happy coincidence. "I can do it, Mrs. Green," I said. "I am a friend of Bobbie's and I am currently looking for a job and a place to live."

Mrs. Green turned her attention toward me and I could feel her eyes checking me out.

"She's very reliable," Bobbie quickly added. "And I can always help out too."

"That would be a great easement," Mrs. Green said. "Come over for tea tomorrow morning and I'll show you girls what you need to do.

"Thank you, Mrs. Green. We'll see you tomorrow." We bounded downstairs as we could hear Mrs. Green opening the door of her apartment. I wondered whether anyone else in New York was as lucky as I seemed to be.

On the way back to the apartment we realized that we still had a little time so we decided to go to the Metropolitan Museum of Art, because Bobbie decided she wanted to show me her favorite painting. It was a painting of Joan of Arc by Jules Bastien-Lepage (1848-1884). The painting titled *Joan of Arc Listening to the Voices* was first exhibited in 1880. It is oil on canvas and measures 100"x110". Bastien-Lepage is probably a lesser known Impressionist painter due to his untimely death at 37 years old.

In the painting Joan, dressed in a peasant girl's clothing, is standing in front of her house and is accompanied by the ethereal images of her visions. The look on her face is one of awe, but it is also tinged with determination, as if she already knows the fate that awaits her.

How could a young peasant girl in 16th century France end up leading an army to victory against the English? Such an unbelievable story and yet it happened. The young girl heard voices that guided her and told her what to do. Do people hear voices today? If so, what are they being told?

I was wondering about this, fascinated by the painting when I noticed that there was an older man standing next to us, also admiring the large canvas in front of us.

"Beautiful, isn't she?" he said.

"Yes, and so enigmatic. Were the voices real?" I found myself asking, as if I knew that he might have the answer.

"Allow me to introduce myself," the man said, lifting his hat. "My name is Doctor Heron, John Heron." We shook hands and I introduced Bobbie to him.

"The fact is that everything speaks to us—perhaps not in English or in human language, but in terms of energy there is a constant transmission from everywhere in the universe and from the energy fields of the planet itself that pass through every human's aura every minute of every day. The voices of our ancestors speak to us and so do the millions of lives that are alive today. Every event, every memory, every person, every animal, plant, mineral and even every inanimate object has its energetic imprint that can be connected to and received, either consciously, semi-consciously or unconsciously. That is what meditation is for—to quiet down enough to listen—to listen to the inner voices as well as to those that are attempting to reach us from outside.

In·sight: MOMENTS OF BEING

"Ghosts do exist. They are energetic scars in the energy field of the planet, sometimes referred to as the astral light. Here everything that has ever happened on planet Earth is stored and retained. If something dramatic occurs, like a murder or a battle, the energetic imprint of that event is stronger than anything else that has ever taken place in that vicinity and so it will become a record which is easier to connect to than, say, a single thought or a casual conversation. There are many stories of people reconnecting to the past in places where historic and dramatic events have taken place. These are places where the veil between the seen and the unseen, the material and energetic worlds wears thin.

"The record of a place, even if not dramatic, is still there, and someone who is sensitive or attuned to a particular frequency, can pick it up and intuitively feel it. That is why we can respond to different atmospheres in different homes, places and historic sites—sometimes feeling well and energized, while other times we might feel tired and drained. There are places we would rather not frequent, which are incompatible with our own energy and vibration—places where we would rather not visit. Someone else, on the other hand, might feel perfectly at home in such a place, simply because their human radio set is tuned in to a frequency that is on a similar wavelength.

"Did Joan hear voices? Undoubtedly. Were they really the voices of the Virgin Mary and the saints? Sometimes we cloak frequencies we feel and receive according to our upbringing, education, knowledge and religion. That is why people of different religions, when going through a near death experience, say that they had seen a bright light and depending on their background, they might report being in the presence of Jesus Christ, Mohammed, Buddha or Jehovah. How come Christians don't see Krishna or Buddhists are not summoned into the presence of Christ? Joan heard voices of saints she knew—she had to have a name to recognize who was speaking to her; otherwise she would not have been able to trust her voices and respond to their promptings.

"So who or what really spoke to her? Perhaps we will never know. But the fact is that in hearing her voices and responding to their commands, a simple peasant girl altered the course of history.

"We all have our voices—they speak to us all the time, but mostly we do not listen. In our busy days we seldom have time to stop and virtually eavesdrop upon what that little voice within—our in-tuition—might be saying. Its advice might be, 'Don't go there' or 'Let's try something new.' How often, when a mishap occurs, do we remember and say to ourselves, 'I knew that would happen!'

"Joan's voices cost her her life and she died a painful and horrific death, being burnt at the stake. If she had not listened, she would probably live to an old age in her home village of Domrémy. She would probably marry and have children, as most of her childhood friends eventually did. Her young life cut short, we will never know whether she would have been of some account and immortalized by history books without the urging of her voices.

"It is curious how in times of historic turbulence and change, often a single person who at other times might not have distinguished themselves at all, rises up, takes up the challenge and changes the status quo forever. Winston Churchill was such a person during the Second World War and so was Gandhi, whose actions precipitated the liberation of India from the British Raj. It is almost as if the forces of progress and change recruit someone to champion their goals and the next step in human evolution can happen. We all are capable of taking on the challenge tomorrow presents to us. But to respond to it we must be able to be quiet inside and to listen.

"We also need to know that not all voices are promoting high connections and human evolution. Every level of energy wants to continue to exist and to grow. Every emotion and quality, every thought and feeling that has been manufactured and processed by humans since people have walked this Earth, still exists within the astral light or akashic records of the planet. They all wish to continue and are always looking for people who are on their wavelength and who might offer them a renewed chance to develop and grow. So patience is looking for patient people or for those who are open to being patient, even if they would not describe themselves as particularly patient. Indeed, patience visits hospitals where patients are told they need time to heal. This is an important concept, for once understood, it will allow a person to connect to any quality or feeling they wish, providing they can put themselves on its frequency and open themselves to its calling card. Courage is looking for courage, integrity for integrity and peace for peace. A behavior that is attuned to a particular quality is a good way to attract that essence from the outside in. So someone who is afraid and shaking in their boots, but despite it are still prepared to act courageously, will attract courage. The next time they call upon courage to attend them, it will respond that much faster, recognizing its new host. Every time a person connects to a quality, even for a brief moment, some of that quality will rub off on them and stay with them until called upon. If witnessed by others, their behavior will be confirmed many times over and others will start speaking about that person in terms of being courageous, for example.

"The thoughts of others carry a charge, so that when they think of us we can sometimes feel it. If others start thinking of us as having high qualities, we can become confirmed and blessed, and our qualities are enhanced. But this can also be to our detriment if what others think of us are negative thoughts that might take away from our desire and effort to develop and grow."

We listened to Doctor Heron for about half an hour. Finally, we realized it was getting late and we needed to get back.

"Nice to meet you," we said.

"You might be interested in the fact that there is also a statue of Joan of Arc here in New York," Doctor Heron said. We both looked at him in surprise.

"Oh yes," he explained. "The statue is located at the west end of 93rd Street within the Joan of Arc Island, which is an adjunct to Riverside Park, situated across Riverside Drive, east of the Henry Hudson Parkway.

"The Statue of Saint Joan was sculpted by Anna Vaughn Hyatt

Huntington. It stands high on a hill overlooking the Hudson River. This was the first public statue in the city to be dedicated to a woman (as opposed to idealized concepts such as Liberty and Victory). The statue depicts Joan on a horse, with her sword raised, ready for battle, with her eyes on the sword. With the other hand she is holding the reins of the horse.

"The pedestal of the sculpture was designed by the architect John Van Pelt. It has ornate columned arches cut in stone, reminiscent of the historical period when Joan was alive. The statue was funded by the Joan of Arc committee which raised funds to commemorate the 500th anniversary of her birth. There are four copies of the statue in other parts of the world. Go and see it. You'll like it," Doctor Heron added.

When we got back I looked up the history of Joan of Arc on the Internet. I found out that Joan of Arc was a peasant girl from the village of Domrémy in the duchy of Bar, which was loyal to France, even though it was surrounded by Burgundian territory. She was born in 1412 during the One Hundred Years' war, which began in 1337 as a dispute over succession to the French throne and lasted until 1453.

When Joan was 12 she began to see visions and hear voices which she consequently identified as the voices of the saints Michael, Catherine and Margaret. The voices urged her to drive out the English who were in alliance with Philip the Good, Duke of Burgundy. In her vision Joan was also persuaded to bring Charles, the Dauphin, to Reims to be crowned king.

At the age of 17 Joan was granted an audience with the Dauphin at the French court in Chinon. She arrived in male disguise and received permission to travel to Orléans at the head of a military relief expedition. After five months of siege by the English, Orléans was weakened, but with several attacks led by Joan, the English lifted the siege.

The course of the war was reversed and the French army marched to Reims where Charles VII was crowned. In 1430 Joan was captured by the Burgundians and sold to the English. She was tried for heresy at Rouen, the seat of the English occupational government and was burned at the stake on May 30th, 1431. She was only 19 years old. Joan was canonized in 1920 by Pope Benedict XV and became Saint Joan—one of the most popular saints of all time.

May 30th became her saint's day and by some curious coincidence we had been admiring the painting of Joan and wondering about her life on the anniversary of her death—it was May 30th.

That afternoon I had my first interview with The Healthy Gourmet. I prepared my application and resumé, and a couple of references as well as my college certificate, and went to meet the interviewer. When I got to the building on 42nd Street, I had a curious feeling that I had been there before, although there was no way that could have been true as this was my first visit to New York.

Once I arrived on the 11th floor, I was surprised to see about a dozen women of all ages sitting in the reception area, obviously also waiting for an interview. I approached the receptionist and she added my name to the list.

"There are fourteen people to be interviewed ahead of you," she said, "but it is going quickly. There are three interviewers," she added. "Some people have gone for a walk, but I would suggest you stay here."

A moment later a young man and an older woman came into the reception area. The woman left by the main entrance while the man walked over to the reception desk, picked up the list and called out a name. "Mrs. Wilson," he said. A young woman with dark hair and glasses on very high heals got up from a chair in the middle of the reception area and followed the young man down a corridor to the right. I quickly occupied the vacant chair. Soon an older woman came out into the reception area and another name was called. The receptionist was right; the process was going quickly.

My turn came about 20 minutes later. I was summoned by the third interviewer—an older man wearing a corduroy jacket and sporting a graying mustache. When we arrived at his office, I noticed he had a grand view of the Grand Central Terminal from the window and that there was a photograph of a happy family on his desk—he was much younger in the photograph and he was standing next to a pretty young woman and two smiling children—a boy holding a large ball and a girl wearing braces on her teeth.

"Beautiful family," I said as I sat down in front of his desk and he took his place behind the desk. I also noticed the name plaque on the desk—it spelled Martin Conlan. He waved his hand. "That's an old picture," he said. "The children are all grown up and have moved away to different corners of the world. Time goes so quickly."

I handed him my papers. He sat there for a moment, reading my resumé.

"We are looking for three things in our employees—" he said, "discipline, initiative and loyalty. Do you think you have what it takes?"

"Absolutely," I replied with conviction. "In fact, those are the very qualities that I have often been told I possess. The first two you mentioned—discipline and initiative—are mentioned in my references."

Martin shuffled through my papers and read the reference from my previous employer, which was a large company importing and selling furniture.

"Yes, I see," he said. "And what do you expect from an employer?" he then asked.

"I expect fairness and quality," I replied. "I also want to work for a company that is sensitive to the environment and promotes good health. I see that your company does that. People need good foods and an education about which foods are good for them."

Martin smiled. "You are absolutely right," he said. "Well, let me tell you a little bit more about The Healthy Gourmet. We buy and sell only the best foods and we are constantly looking for new recipes and ingredients from all over the world. We are also looking for new markets. The job might involve some research and sales. Are you interested in learning a whole new area of expertise? I see you were in the furniture business before."

"I am totally interested in good food," I replied. "I might have worked for a furniture company, but in my own life I have always been interested in eating well. I believe we are responsible for the sanctity of our own bodies and what we put in our mouths is very important—it can make us healthy or wreak havoc with our inner lives."

Martin put down the papers he was holding and looked at me intently for a moment, without saying a word. Finally he spoke. "You're right," he said and with that simple sentence he got up. "We will be in touch," he said. He extended his hand over the desk and I got up as well. As I shook his hand, an image came into my mind of a young woman being slapped by an angry man. Somehow I knew their names.

"Tell Jennifer she should be careful about becoming too involved with George. He has a history of violent behavior," I said. Martin looked at me incredulously with his mouth open. He was speechless and I couldn't help smiling at the sight of his dumb-struck expression.

"Bye," I said and quickly turned around to hide my grin and headed for the door.

Chapter Six

Compassion

That night I dreamed I was in a large building complex which was part of the old mystery school where the Master was the teacher. Again, I had the feeling I had been there before, perhaps in another lifetime or in my dreams. Everything looked familiar and it felt like coming home.

In my dream I was staying in a guest room located in one of the annex buildings adjacent to the main house. I was awoken early in the morning and told that a car was waiting to take me to the site of the next test. I sat in the back of the car with a different driver in front. The driver was a man in his forties and as we drove away, he informed me that he would be briefing me on the way about the day ahead. The drive seemed to take a long time and as the sun slowly climbed higher in the sky, we reached some hills and then a range of mountains, outlined in grey-green against the summer sky.

"Today's test is a test of endurance," the driver said. "You will need to climb a steep incline and walk along quite a dangerous precipice. I hope you are fit."

"I think I am," I said, feeling my heart begin to beat faster in anticipation of the day's events.

"It won't take all day," he continued, "because I will be driving you back before sundown. But you will need to pace yourself and be very aware of your surroundings." And then, as if in reply to a mute question from me, he added, "There is no danger of getting lost; the trail is clearly marked."

The road was now beginning to wind through the foothills of the mountains, serpentining its way higher and higher until, at last, the majestic scenery came closer and I could feel that our destination was near. Just at the highest point the road seemed to dip lower again, leading into the valley that previously I could see from the summit of the hill. It was a large green valley with a river running through it, covered in orchards and fields, with a few villages scattered along the banks of the river. As the car started to descend, the sun suddenly became overshadowed by the mountain looming on the eastern side of the valley, while the other side remained bathed in glittering light.

"We are almost there," said the driver as he guided the car across a small rickety bridge towards the other side of the valley. From there the road started to ascend again, leading up a zigzag path to higher elevations. At the second or third bend, there was a small rest area with a couple of cars already parked on the paved surface.

"This is it," he said. "This is where it starts." He pulled in and parked the car. He climbed out of the driver's seat and opened the door for me. I got out, stretching my arms and legs, glad to be standing on firm ground again. He then walked around to the trunk of the car and pulled out a backpack. As he handed it to me, he said, "There's water in here and a few snacks to keep you going. Follow the blue trail and I will be waiting for you at the other end. Good luck!"

"Thank you," I said, wondering what it was all supposed to mean. Having come this far, I realized there was nothing else I could do but to wander on my way and discover what there was to discover. I looked behind me and saw the driver get back into the car and pull out from the small parking lot on the side of the road. I then looked ahead and saw that I was standing by the road, looking across at a wooded area covering quite a steep incline. On one of the trees there was a blue marking and I then noticed a narrow path leading in between the trees. Well, at least I had a starting point, I thought, as I ventured among the pines. It suddenly became quite cold and gloomy, as the sun had no way of penetrating through the dense branches. However, the path was clearly laid out and I could follow it with ease. The incline was not as steep as it initially looked from the road and I decided to make good haste while the going was this easy.

As I climbed I began to hear various sounds—the rustle of leaves and the breaking of dead twigs under foot, the calls of birds and the occasional scurry of a small animal. As the incline steepened, my pace slowed down. The forest around me became more dense and the path more narrow and it almost felt as if it would go on forever. There were narrow streams with water trickling downhill, many varieties of pine and spruce, bushes with berries and logs to climb over as they lay across the path. As I climbed further uphill, I noticed that I was getting out of breath, so I paused for a moment and took a drink of water from my backpack.

Then, as I started climbing again along a rather steep incline I noticed light appearing through the trees. I hastened my step despite the fact that I was getting tired, and the light increased; I realized I was reaching the end of the forest. And then suddenly, at the brow of the hill, the forest abruptly ended and I was standing at the edge of a clearing with grass and flowers stretching as far as the eye could see. From here there was a dip in the terrain descending on the other side of the hill and then a grassy incline indicated by blue markings on occasional rocks, leading up a mountain that towered over the valley in front of me. I could see the narrow path disappearing around the side of the mountain as it steeply inclined toward the summit. Gathering my strength, I proceeded on, downhill and then up, up and up. When I finally reached the part of the path that was winding in an ascending spiral around the mountain, the view opened up again and I was about to walk along a rocky ledge, with a dramatic perpendicular drop several hundred feet below. The drop ended in rocks and stones and further beyond I could see the valley with the river and the orchards and the green fields along its banks.

I proceeded with caution, keeping to the mountain side of the path, trying not to look at what lay below. I decided to take my time and make sure that my foot would not slip on one of the many stones and boulders strewn upon the path I was following. I knew, of course, that this too was a test and decided to pass it with flying colors. I felt that caution was the key and was already beginning to imagine my successful completion of the task, when suddenly I heard a voice calling out. I could hardly believe my ears. Just along the path, a short distance ahead of where I was, someone had clearly slipped and fell, but was still holding on to the ledge. I could only see the hands, the knuckles white with effort and strain, and a male voice, crying out, "Help, help me." I ran up to the place where the fall had occurred and carefully peered over the edge of the cliff. It was a young man and he was holding on to dear life, trying to find a grip with his feet, but in vain, as the rock face at that point was as smooth as a sheet of glass. I could see his eyes and the fear and panic which had set in, as he was facing inevitable death. Then, as I approached and he saw my head appearing over the ledge, he looked relieved and there was hope in his voice, as he commanded, "Give me your hand. You can pull me up."

I quickly assessed the situation. He was a large man, strong and muscular and I had nothing to hold on to.

"You will pull me down with you," I said and instinctively I knew that I would not have the strength to pull him up.

"Just give me your hand," he insisted, as his fingers started to slip away from the edge. His voice grew even more insistent. "I can't hold on much longer. Give me your hand." His voice was quieter now, more pleading; begging almost.

"I can't," I said, and repeated again, "I can't. I don't want to die with you. If I give you my hand, you will surely pull me down with you."

The man couldn't hear my last words, because as I was uttering them, his fingers slipped away and he lost his grip. I could clearly see him fall several feet and I could hear the thud as he fell onto a pile of rocks below.

I lay down on the path to look over the edge and saw him lying there, his body in a lifeless heap as he was motionlessly draped over a large protruding boulder. I waited several seconds for a sign of life—a movement of a limb or the sound of a moan, but could hear and see nothing. There was no doubt about it—the man was dead. This was the first death I had ever seen in my life, apart from being a witness on the day my grandmother had passed away, and I felt that I had contributed to its occurrence. I sat down on the path to gather myself together and think through what had just happened. I was upset and worried that this event would be a mark against me on my journey. I wished I could have somehow saved him but didn't know how. I had always believed in the sanctity of life and in the need to help others, but in this situation I had chosen my own life over and above the possibility of helping another. But could I have helped him? There was no way I would have had the strength to pull the man away from the precipice. It is true that I could have chosen to die with him rather than feel this terrible remorse that I now felt. But what good would that have done? Wasn't my first responsibility to protect my own life before I could offer a helping hand to another human being?

With these persistent thoughts spinning around my head, I slowly got up to my feet. After all, I still had a task to perform and needed to be on my way if I was to finish before sunset. But somehow this whole charade seemed to be pointless now as I slowly continued along the path, lost in thoughts. What reward could there possibly be in earning my so-called development, if a man had died in agony because of my callousness? Maybe there was a way, after all, in which I could have helped. I looked back toward the spot from which the man had fallen in search of something to hold on to, but there was nothing. Up here at these elevations the ground was as barren as a desert, parched by the wind and the sun, with only rocks, stones and boulders interrupting the monotony of the mountain pass.

I walked on with a heavy burden on my shoulders. Soon the path circled the mountain face to reveal a new vista where I would lose from sight the scene of the recent tragedy. As I turned around the bend, I saw a lonely figure, sitting on a rock, looking into the distance. As I approached, I recognized the Master and hastened my step as I prepared to meet him. I felt such a mixture of emotions gripping me as I came closer—joy mingled with sadness, remorse and expectation, excitement and despair, all at once. I found myself almost running toward him, with tears streaming down my face. As I approached, he slowly turned toward me, carefully examining me with his eyes—his face quite expressionless, as if waiting to hear from me first. I stopped in front of him, dropped my bag to the ground and sat on the path in front of him. As I spoke, my voice sounded tearful and upset.

"There was a man back there... I wanted to help him, but he fell... I didn't know how... I couldn't... I wish I had..."

He smiled. Smiled! A human tragedy was playing out before him and he was smiling. I couldn't believe it.

"You've said the magic words—you wish you had helped. In that case you will be granted something that does not often happen in life. You will be given a second chance. Now go back and help him."

I looked at him incredulously. How could this be? The man was dead, I saw his contorted body, I had heard him fall; I was a witness to a tragedy. But at the same time I knew better than to argue with the Master. So I silently got up, turned around and started walking back along the path toward the spot where the fateful fall had occurred. As I circumnavigated the bend, the precipice came clearly into view and yet again I could hear the man's cries and I could see his fingers, holding on with difficulty to the rock ledge. I rushed toward him, convinced that this was someone else, and as I approached, I could see the face of the same man, strained with effort and exasperation. This felt like being in a movie that has been rewound or in a strange dream and I couldn't believe my eyes, but there was no time to try and figure it out.

"Help me, help me," he shouted as he spotted me and I wondered if somehow time had been reversed for this moment to be able to repeat itself. There was no turning back for me, although I still had my doubts whether I could help the man pull himself back over the edge. He would undoubtedly take me with him to his death below. But as I had found myself inside a miracle, I decided that I would rise to the occasion and fulfill my own wish to help. I was preparing myself to die as I lay down on the path.

"Hold on," I said and I stretched my right hand out to him. I could feel him grasp it with his left hand, as he let go of the ledge, still holding on with the fingers of his right hand. I expected to be slowly pulled over the edge; he was still holding on with his right hand and I was beginning to stretch my left arm toward him when my hand came across an obstacle—something hard and firm. I grasped the object without looking, as I was still staring into the man's eyes. It felt like a young tree with its uneven bark, holding fast underneath my fingers. Now I had some resistance, I began to pull the man's arm. It gave way, as he was helping with his other hand, pushing against the hard surface of the rock. And so, pulling and pushing, I was soon kneeling and his head and shoulders emerged above the edge of the precipice. A few more inches and a few more moments of struggle and I was inching my way away from the edge. Soon he brought his right leg forward and there he was—kneeling in front of me on the path. I could hardly believe my eyes, but we were now both level with each other, with a young pine tree between us. We both felt relief and joy and for a brief moment we fell into each other's arms, laughing and crying at the same time. A moment later, we pulled away from each other, embarrassed at the sudden display of emotion.

"Thank you, thank you. I thought I was a dead man..."

"You were," I replied, and then added, "the tree was not there before..."

"No, I don't remember it either."

"How could that be?"

We slowly got up, brushing the mountain dust off our clothes. He looked at me and said, "I was walking too fast. I slipped on a rock. You saved my life."

"No, I didn't," I objected. "The tree did."

He laughed and repeated, "I owe my life to you."

"You owe me nothing," I said. "I better be on my way. Goodbye."

"Goodbye and thank you. I hope one day someone helps you as selflessly as you have helped me."

In·sight: MOMENTS OF BEING

I smiled as we shook hands, and then I slowly walked away. I felt embarrassed that I had not helped him before and wished to hide my embarrassment. As I returned to the spot where the Master had been sitting on a rock, I saw my bag in exactly the same spot on which I had left it a few moments before. I picked it up and continued on my way, following the blue markings along the path. Soon the trail began to descend toward the valley below and I was able to quicken my step. It did not take long for me to reach the trees and follow the path back into the forest that was covering the lower elevations of the mountain. I could feel that it was getting to be quite late, as the temperature dropped among the trees. I moved faster still and soon I could see that I was coming to the bottom of the mountain, as the trees became more sparse and the afternoon sun began to penetrate between the branches. Finally I came out of the forest onto a field and the path led me through the field and onto a road which ran along the other side of the field. There I spotted three men sitting on a bench, as if they were waiting for me—the Master, the driver and the man I had rescued only a short while before.

"Yes, it's me," he said when he saw my surprise. "I played a part in your tasking."

And then the Master spoke, "You needed to experience compassion. You also needed to learn that when it comes to helping another, there is always assistance available and that you can't compute the odds against you or for you in those situations. You needed to learn that helping another is a requirement upon you and that you must place greater value upon the life of another. Life is a gift and it is sacred, wherever and whenever you come across it. Preserving life is a sacred duty and today you have fulfilled that duty."

I tried to protest, but he raised his hand, as if to silence me and continued, "Today you were given a second chance. This can only happen once. It will not happen again."

With that he turned to the driver and indicating the car with his hand, he said: "And now you can take her back."

The driver obediently stood up and opened the back door of the car for me. I responded to his gesture and soon we were on our way.

Chapter Seven

Cleopatra's Needle

The next day I moved downstairs. It was the easiest move I had ever accomplished—two suitcases down two flights of stairs. Mrs. Green was packed and ready to go. She had ordered a taxi and was keen to show me everything before it was time to leave. The most important information (according to her) was where the cat food was kept and the respective feeding bowls and feeding times. She obviously loved her cats and took good care of them. I promised I would do the same.

She also showed me where I should sleep, where she kept the linen, the mop and vacuum cleaner. She also explained that I would need to go to the basement to do the laundry or visit the laundromat around the corner.

A quick tour around the small kitchen and I became familiar with the cupboards where pots, pans, dishes and cans of food were kept. Considering her supplies, it looked like I would not need to spend too much on food during her absence.

"You can eat anything that is in the fridge, the freezer or the cupboards," she said. "It will all be too old to eat by the time I get back." A moment later the buzzer rang and the taxi driver had arrived. I helped her with her bags and waved her off, as the taxi pulled out from in front of the building.

So now I had an apartment all to myself. I walked back upstairs and turned on my laptop computer. I felt lucky to be alive and to be in a city where everything is possible. I believed it was possible to achieve anything one desired there.

I checked my emails and the first thing I noticed was a message from The Healthy Gourmet inviting me back for a second interview. This time I would be meeting the president of the company and his assistant. I was thrilled. I had not yet had my other two interviews and already I was being asked back to see the president of The Healthy Gourmet.

To celebrate this happy turn of events I walked over to Central Park. It was a beautiful day and there were flowers in bloom everywhere. People were out with their dogs, their children and their friends. Joggers were jogging, bikers were biking and all seemed good with the world.

Behind the Metropolitan Museum of Art I came across Cleopatra's needle. I walked up the little hillock it is located on and stood within its presence. I could definitely feel something—an aura of peace and wellbeing. I somehow sensed that it was aligned to the sun as the rays of the sun seemed especially powerful in its vicinity, almost as though I was on the top of a mountain where air is rarified and solar rays can penetrate the atmosphere more effectively.

As I was admiring the ancient edifice and pondering about its origin, I noticed a man who was standing on the other side of the obelisk. I felt his eyes on me and I looked at him inquisitively. He took a few steps in my direction.

"Powerful, isn't it?" he asked.

"Yes, it is. I can feel it," I replied.

"Then you are sensitive to atmospheres," he said. "Of course, it's not Cleopatra's and it's not a needle. Peacefully located on a mound behind the Metropolitan Museum, it is a testimony to the very advanced civilization that was ancient Egypt. Where did they come from? Speculations continue today. New evidence is being uncovered all the time. One of the latest revelations confirms that the sphinx is much older than Egyptologists had surmised and that it had suffered from water erosion—clearly before

Sahara was a desert. Books have been written about the origins of the ancient Egyptian culture and scientists have argued about its beginnings for decades.

"Two theories persist, though neither has been proven. One is that the ancient Egypt that we know of has no preceding culture that could explain its arising. It suggests that Egypt was built by extraterrestrial visitors who arrived here from a distant planet or a star, bringing their knowledge and their culture with them. The other suggests that indeed there was a previous civilization which gave rise to ancient Egypt and other advanced cultures around the world, before it was destroyed and all traces of it disappeared. This could be Atlantis or Lemuria, but, again, there is no proof as yet that such a place existed. Was Plato's description of Atlantis based on fact or was it a utopia that he envisioned and described?

"The fact is that the Egyptian culture arose and thrived within the Nile valley long before any signs of Rome or Greece were heard of. The artistry and evidence of the technology and skills of early Egyptian builders and craftsmen have survived until today to baffle scientists and historians alike.

"To understand more about Egypt, one would need to become sensitive to the unseen worlds of energy. Egyptian times and culture were very different to ours. Their atmospheres were semi-conductive and they were trained to see, feel and understand energies. The obelisk is an antenna—a device to transmit and receive energies. That's why you are feeling the power of the sun more acutely. This hill is a place where one can more easily connect to higher powers. I come here to meditate and contemplate about ancient mysteries that are still alive today.

"Isn't it curious how the great cities of the Western World—London, Paris, Istanbul, New York and Washington—all have an obelisk? What could have promoted the city planners to import such great and powerful monoliths into the hearts of each of these cities? Was it indeed a Masonic conspiracy as some theorists suggest?"

The man paused and, is if remembering something, he said, "So sorry. Allow me to introduce myself. My name is Richard Raven."

Mr. Raven had raven black hair and raven dark eyes. When I looked into his eyes, I felt I could keep looking forever. Realizing I was beginning to stare, I looked away.

"How do you know all this?" I asked.

"I study energies," he said. "Egyptians knew all about human energies and their whole civilization was based upon this knowledge. If they met someone, they would be more interested in their energetic content than their looks. In fact, in early Egypt they would choose their king according to his illumination. They had this glass paste that only a special kind of human could light up, simply by their energetic radiation, thus displaying their energetic content. So a king, who ruled Egypt before the pharaohs, was not a hereditary function but was chosen according to his ability to light up a pectoral made of this glass paste."

"That's amazing! Who taught you all this?"

"I belonged to a mystery school that was modeled after the mystery schools of Egypt. This knowledge is still being passed on from generation to generation. Look at the obelisk. See how the tip is shining and emitting energy?" I could see the sun being reflected in the tip of the obelisk; I wasn't so sure about the energy.

"I see it shines," I replied. "Is that energy or a reflection of the sun?" I looked back at Mr. Raven and into those almond-shaped eyes.

"No, no. You have to change the way you look at something. You are used to focusing—at school you were taught to focus on a book, a blackboard, a teacher. Try now to un-focus your eyes. Look at me. He was standing with his back to the obelisk. I did what he said and I could see a tall, good-looking man with an obelisk in the background. "Now look just above my head," he said. He raised his hand to a spot a few inches above his head and I looked at his hand.

"Now look through my hand," he carried on with the instructions. "Look through the obelisk, through the park and through New York, all the way to the Atlantic ocean and to the horizon. This is the eternal look of the sphinx." He brought his hand down, while I continued to look, un-focusing my eyes. As soon as I had done so, I gasped. A faint light formed up around his head and shoulders and, as far as I could see, while still looking above his head, all the way down to the ground. I continued to look and it grew brighter. In fact, I thought I could see a color—it was light blue and shimmering."

"You can see it!" he exclaimed. "I can tell because you gasped at the sight. Can you see a color?"

"I can," I replied. "I can see blue."

"That's right! I was thinking blue. I projected it into my aura."

I tried to focus on the blue color to see if I could better tell the shade of blue, but immediately the bright light disappeared.

"Don't focus," Mr. Raven exclaimed, "or you will lose it."

"I already did," I said.

"You need to practice. You can do this at home. Just place a plant in front of a light background. The plant has what is called an etheric too. Everything living does." He took a few steps away from the obelisk and came up to me.

"Let's try something else. I will show you an Egyptian posture that will send a surge of energy through your body and your energy field. That will help you see into the worlds of energy and power." He instructed me to copy him as he brought one foot forward, raised his shoulders and rolled them back and down. He then brought his fingers together and held his hands by his side with the palms pointing behind him. Finally, he swung his palms to face the hips, rolled his fingers up and projected his thumbs forward. He then instructed me to once again look long distance. As I did so I suddenly felt a tingling in the hands and for a brief moment I felt as if there was a stream of energy coming out of my thumbs.

"That's amazing," I said. "I felt that."

"It's very real," he confirmed as he relaxed his shoulders and I relaxed mine.

"Just look at that tree," he then said pointing in front of him. I turned around and looked at the tree. "Now un-focus your eyes again and maybe you will be able to see something from the energy worlds appear before you."

I tried to look through the tree, through the park and all the way to the horizon. I thought I could see something.

"I see a shimmering light around the tree and around all the trees," I said.

"That's right," he confirmed. I noticed he had a hand on my shoulder. I took a step back and freed myself from his touch. "I've got to go," I said. "Nice meeting you."

"Can I see you again?" he asked. I felt he had been too bold too soon, but I didn't want to be rude.

"Give me your number," I said. "I'll see how things work out." He took out a business card and handed it to me. "Richard Raven, Merlin Magician" it said and it had a phone number. On the other side there was a picture of a raven on a branch of a tree against a blue background.

"Thanks," I said. As I turned away to leave, he called after me: "What is your name? You haven't told me your name!"

"Mary," I replied, turning back toward him. "Mary Dove." I have no idea where that came from or why I said it. The Mary Dove name was certainly not true. I smiled to myself as I walked away. I then noticed, as I thought about the word dove, that there was only one letter of a difference between dove and love. I also wondered why, with some people, I could be reluctant to divulge my real name. I then realized that when you tell someone your name, you are giving them a little bit of your power. Your name is something that accompanies you throughout life, unless, of course, you change it through marriage or in any other way. Every time someone calls your name, whether with endearment or criticism, they are transmitting to you a little bit of their power. The people whose names we remember have a more lasting place in our memory and receive from us our thoughts, images and feelings in a more direct way—when we think of them, that thought travels to them. If it is a positive sentiment, it will add to their supply of confirmation and well-being, but if it is negative, it can be an energetically detrimental experience for them, whether they are aware of it or not.

This might seem odd, but sometimes I could feel other people's thoughts about me. Mostly I tried to deflect them because they were not useful in my development. When, however, I did pick up that someone was sending me positive energy, I felt a sense of wellbeing and joy.

In the case of Richard Raven, I was somewhat concerned that as a self-proclaimed magician who obviously knew about the energy worlds, he might be too eager to send me his thoughts —good or bad—and invade my energy field without asking permission to do so. I felt strongly that energy workers needed a code of conduct and a respect for another person's privacy. Perhaps it was up to me to write one.

Chapter Eight

Value

That evening I felt restless. It was exciting to have my own place, at least for a while, and I also felt that I was learning more and more about energies and the unseen worlds around me. I felt a veil was being lifted and although I had always known that these realms of power and force existed, they were now becoming more real. I was also thinking about Richard Raven and his mysterious knowledge. Although I had left the scene at the obelisk in a hurry, I now felt like I wanted to know more and that perhaps this man was a key to my initiation into ancient mysteries. I hesitated for a while, but then I decided to call him. He answered promptly and did not seem surprised that I was calling him.

"How are you?" he asked.

"I'm fine, but I am very intrigued by your knowledge and ability to connect to unseen power. Is there a school I can attend or a teacher I can study with?" I asked.

"I am a teacher," he replied. "I can teach you but it will take time and discipline before you get any results. You will need patience."

"I have always believed that anything worth having takes effort and time, " I said.

"In that case, let's meet and talk," he suggested and we agreed to meet up the next day.

In·sight: MOMENTS OF BEING

That night my dreams about being in the mystery school continued. I dreamed I was back in the little bedroom, located in the annex building adjacent to the main school building where, apart from a bed, a closet and a table, there was also a desk with a computer on it. When I woke up in the morning within the dream, there was a message on the computer. It said: "Question: What is your most valued possession?"

I then went for a walk within the school grounds and started thinking about the question and in my mind I was examining everything I owned. In surveying my earthly possessions, which I supposedly owned within the dream, the one single, most valuable object, both in monetary terms and in terms of its function in my life and its service to my wellbeing, was what I thought of as my house. In my dream I was thinking about the house I had co-owned when I was married and continued to live in briefly after the divorce. In reality the house had been sold long ago and the proceeds from the sale had all been spent. Even when I lived in the house it was not completely mine because it was partially owned by the bank, as I was still paying a mortgage. However, I considered it mine because it was mine in name, in title and in deed. I thought about that house—probably for the first time since I had moved out of it—with feeling and with appreciation, almost as if it were alive. It kept me warm when it was cold outside and cool when it was hot; it provided me with safety and gave me a place to store and use my belongings; it had kept me dry in rainy weather and housed all the utilities necessary to provide the important facilities of living itself.It allowed me to keep clean and fed and rested. It always felt good walking through the door after a journey, whether long or short. It was decorated the way I liked it—its colors felt right and pleasant to be with. In fact it was my own ecology, my own atmosphere, created by my own hand and it reflected my taste and needs. I could change it any time I wanted to and bring it up to date with my current taste and desires. At that moment I remembered the leaky faucet in the bathroom and the door to the basement which had never been painted, and I felt guilty that I had neglected my house, or rather some aspects of it, thereby not allowing it to be of adequate service to me. Curious

Value

that I was thinking of my house as a living, feeling entity—it felt like a servant or even a friend, always there for me, ready to oblige, even during the most difficult times. And yet, how could I value an inanimate object above all else? Was I becoming sentimental and unrealistic, appreciating comfort and security above the warmth and kindness of a friend?

But the question mentioned possessions, not people or friends, so it no doubt referred to something I owned. Once again in my mind I ran through the catalogue of my possessions as far as I could remember, because here at the school I felt quite detached from the many objects that had filled my house and shared my life.

And then I thought of my cat, Andromeda, whom I had left behind. After all, she was my possession, for I had purchased her two years before in a pet shop. I never intended to have a cat, but once I saw her, I could not leave her in the shop, at the mercy of some future customer who might or might not give her a good home. She had looked at me so pathetically that I could not resist her and decided there and then that I would adopt her and give her a home. Since that day, she had taken to following me around the house and the garden, causing me to stumble over her, and lying on her back in a submissive posture, begging to be rubbed, scratched and petted, the moment I would step through the door. She would sit on my lap during my quiet moments and sleep at the foot of my bed at night. In fact, I could almost feel and sense that she was missing me right now, even though she was being well looked after by Angie, who used to be my next-door neighbor.

I felt quite satisfied with the process so far and decided to have a look at the board where daily activities were being announced. I had just finished breakfast and was wondering how I could usefully spend my time before going to see the Master in the evening with my response to the question which had appeared on my computer screen in the morning. I looked at the notice board and saw that there was going to be an excursion after breakfast into the high mountains that could be seen in the distance, if you looked out the windows on the west side of the school building. It made me think of the day I had climbed the mountain and saved the life of the man who had fallen over the precipice, but this time the excursion was going to be an adventure higher up still, beginning with a cable car ride up to a lower peak, to then continue a climb to higher altitudes.

I went back to my room and changed into my walking shoes and warmer clothing, as the weather and temperature at these lofty heights could be unpredictable and treacherous. I also collected a bottle of water and my camera and walked outside. In front of the building there was a bus waiting for us and a group of us gathered together, waiting to climb on board.

A young man in his thirties opened the door to the bus and stood on the first step, facing us.

"Make sure you are well dressed and wear good shoes," he said. "We cannot be responsible for you if you fall because you are wearing sandals." He looked at a young man in front of him who was indeed wearing sandals. "Please go and change if you want to come along on this trip," he said. "We will wait another five minutes." With that he jumped down onto the ground, making way for us to get on the bus and choose our seats.

The bus was not full but there were several of us getting on and occupying the seats. I sat by the window and watched a few more people run toward the bus to make it on time. A few minutes later we were on our way, driving through a couple of local villages and then into the foothills of the mountains. We then started climbing around sharp bends, increasing our elevation as we progressed. Looking out of the window, I could see the road where we had come from, as it twisted and turned up the mountainside.

As we continued, the air got colder and several times I had to swallow to unblock my ears. Finally we reached our destination—a small cable car station halfway up the mountain with cable car wires traveling up toward the peak. We disembarked and gathered together. The bus driver stood in front of the group.

"We're going up to the summit in the cable car," he said, pointing to the mountain behind him. "And from there we will start climbing higher." We all looked at the peak behind the mountain in front of us. Its summit was

Value

veiled by clouds and you could see that there was snow and ice up there. I imagined how cold it must be at that altitude. I looked at my companions and noticed that we were a mixed bunch—all ages and apparently all levels of fitness. Would we make it, I wondered. However, the group was already moving toward the cable car. As the last person entered the metal box, the driver came out from the station's side door, entered the car and the doors closed behind us. A bell rang and the car slowly began to move out of position, gradually being pulled off the ground by powerful cables.

As we left the ground and as I looked down onto the top of trees beneath us, I wondered whether this was a test and whether we would stop in mid air. Others were looking out of the windows as well and there was a hush, which fell over the car. But on we went, higher and higher and soon we arrived safely at our destination. There we disembarked and gathered together, admiring the impressive view of snow-capped mountains all around us and awaiting further instructions.

"This is a saddle," our driver and guide explained as we looked toward a brief descent, leading to a higher peak behind the first one which the cable car had brought us to. "We will continue to climb over the scree until we get to the ice field at the top." He started to lead us toward the next mountain top. The air felt cold and fresh and we were all buttoning up our jackets and putting on hats as we went, trying to keep warm. As we reached the other side of the saddle and started the ascent, I suddenly felt light-headed and dizzy. But I didn't want to say anything, in case the guide would ask me to turn back, so I carried on. But I began to feel worse and worse, with nausea and a headache compounding my un-comfortability. I noticed I was not the only one slowing down—the air here was rarified and my breathing became shallow and fast, until I realized I could go no further, as it was a struggle just being able to catch my next breath. I stopped in my tracks, breathing heavily and expecting to be sick. A young man in a blue sports jacket and with good climbing boots which supported his ankles, as well as his feet, approached me and said, "It's the mountain air. It is very rarified here and there is always someone who just cannot take it. I'll take you back."

The others were already disappearing out of sight as they moved on up the winding path. I could see their silhouettes snaking their way on the ascent toward the ice field. I could go no further; I could hardly breathe. With every breath I felt glad I was still alive. I wasn't sure at that moment that I would even make it down.

"Here, take my arm," the young man said and I gladly obliged. I couldn't speak, as I was taking in large gulps of air with every breath. We started to walk back and I was heavily leaning on his arm as we did so.

I only started feeling slightly better as we climbed onto the cable car going down. And then with every minute I felt relief until halfway down, as the car passed the car going up, I finally felt I could speak again.

"Thank you for coming back with me," I said. "I am sorry you missed the climb because of me."

"Oh no, don't be," the young man said. "I went up specifically to help anyone who might be in trouble. You see, it's the altitude and if you are not used to it, you can have trouble breathing. People who live in the mountains have a different constitution and their blood adapts to the nature of the air out there. On these excursions there is always someone who needs to go back. Today it was you, but it could be anyone. It's that simple."

I took a deep breath and filled my lungs with delicious air. "It sure makes me value the air we breathe," I said as the cable car gently reached its destination and came to a stop at its resting station.

That evening when I went to see the Master, I had my answer ready. I entered his study; he was waiting for me, sitting in his usual chair.

"I most value the air, for without it I could not carry on living," I said.

"Then you have learned today's lesson well," he said, "because everything else you have thought about is only an illusion. You cannot possess anything, for what you think you possess, possesses you. The air is food for you, more valuable than the food you eat because you cannot live without it for more than a few minutes. And yet it is freely given to you, which is why it is mostly not valued at all. Also, you cannot see it, and humans mostly do not value what they cannot see, for they have greed in their eyes. They also do not value what they do not pay for. Learn therefore to value the simple things and the fact of living day by day and you will be rich beyond measure. The air is always there for you, so think about the care and generosity of that which has put it there for you to breathe. And when you contemplate those unseen supports that help maintain your life, don't forget the greatest support of all—the energy that is all around you and the sunlight without which humans would perish. Have value therefore for the planet and the sun. They are your second mother and father; this unique universal system is designed to allow human life to flourish and grow."

Chapter Nine

The News Building

The Healthy Gourmet was located near Grand Central Station on 42nd Street. When I arrived on the 11th floor the receptionist asked me to wait. "Mr. Banch is seeing someone else," she said. I sat down on the sofa in the reception area and told her I would be glad to wait.

A few minutes later the girl spoke to me again. "So you're being interviewed for my job?" she asked, though it really came across as a statement, not a question.

"Yes," I replied, "I think so," though I still wasn't quite sure that was the job they were considering me for. "How many candidates are they seeing?" I asked.

"Oh, they've reduced the list down to four. You are the third one today."

"Oh," I replied. I didn't have much else to say. I picked up a leaflet that was lying on the coffee table in front of me. "The Healthy Gourmet" it proclaimed and there was the company logo: a large green celery stalk that looked more like a tree than a vegetable, held by two smiling people on either side. The leaflet described the range of foods sold by The Healthy Gourmet—there was a large selection of preserves of various kinds, nuts, oils, dried fruit, vegetable spreads, including hummus, tapenade and the like.

"We deliver foods all over the country," the receptionist said, as she watched me looking at the brochure. We have warehouses in five states, but not in New York." I looked at her inquisitively and she soon obliged with further information. "Too expensive," she said. "The nearest warehouse is in New Jersey," she added. At that moment the phone rang. She picked up the receiver.

"You can go in now," she said to me. "They're expecting you. First door on the left." She waved in the direction of a pair of glass doors leading to a large corridor. I wasn't sure who "they" were but I knew I would soon find out. I stood in front of the door she had indicated, gathering myself before knocking. I reapplied my lipstick and smoothed down my hair. Then I knocked.

"Enter," I heard and I opened the door. I entered a large office. There was a man sitting behind a desk and a woman standing next to him.

The man stood up. "My name is Henry Banch and this is Mrs. Grey, my assistant. I shook hands with both of them. As I held the woman's hand I felt a sharp pain in my lungs. I squeezed her hand a little harder, trying to understand better what I was feeling. She quickly withdrew her hand. "Mrs. Grey is leaving so today we are recruiting people for two jobs: the receptionist and an assistant to the CEO. Have a seat."

Mrs. Grey was looking at me intently. "I felt that," she said. "It was like an electric shock."

"I'm sorry," I said. "It must be the static."

"No, no," she replied. "It was much stronger than static. It felt more like being connected to a source of energy."

"Let's get down to business," Mr. Banch said. I'm looking at your application," he added as he picked up the form from his desk. "I see you have experience dispatching furniture. Would you be comfortable organizing food deliveries, making travel arrangements and setting up conferences and sales meetings?"

"Yes, certainly," I replied. "I think I could manage that very well."

"What do you know about health foods?" he asked again.

"Well, I try to keep myself healthy by having a balanced diet, eating organic foods and supplements," I said.

"Have you seen our line of products?"

"Yes, and the list is impressive. Do you sell online as well?"

"Most of our sales are done online. But we also deliver to health food stores, food stores and restaurants all over the country. There is a growing demand for health foods."

"Yes, I think people are waking up to the fact that their health depends on what they eat. Out of the four foods, physical food is the most fundamental."

"Four foods?" Mrs. Grey asked. "What do you mean?"

"Well, we take in four kinds of foods that allow us to continue living," I replied. "There is physical food, referred to by the ancient sages as earth food. Then there is liquid food, or water foods, air food and energy. We can survive for several weeks without physical food, but only a few days without liquids and only a few minutes without air. However, without energy we would be dead immediately."

"Interesting," Mrs. Grey replied.

"We do sell water," Mr. Banch said. "We don't package air yet, but maybe one day we will. As for energy, we sell energy bars and energy drinks, but not energy on its own." He chuckled and then stood up. He extended his hand.

"Thank you for coming in, Miss Faye," he said. "We will be in touch."

"Thank you," I replied. I was not sure if the interview had gone well or not. It did seem rather short. I turned around and left the office.

Back in the lobby the receptionist asked me how it had gone. "That was a very short interview," she said.

"Yes, I have no idea how it went," I replied. I was just about to leave when Mrs. Grey came into the lobby and approached me. "What happened in there?" she asked. "That felt like a bolt of energy when we shook hands. The pain has gone."

I looked at her surprised. "Was it your lungs that were hurting?" I asked.

"Yes," she replied. "I have lung cancer and that is why I am leaving. I was a smoker for thirty years. But now I am not feeling any pain. I can breathe freely." She took in a deep breath, demonstrating that she had no pain.

"I am sorry," was all I could think of saying. "I hope you get better soon," I added.

After I left The Healthy Gourmet and started walking toward Grand Central Terminal, I noticed that I was standing in front of the News Building which I recognized from the Superman movie. I decided to go in.

Located at 220 East 42nd Street, I knew that the lobby of the News Building is a must for anyone interested in astronomy or geography.

In the lobby of the News Building one can find an enormous globe representing our planet. There are also indicators as to the distance from 42nd Street where it stands to many major cities of the world, showing the number of miles a person visiting the building is at distance from Bangkok, Tokyo or Toronto, as they stand in front of the globe. There is also information about our galaxy—distances between planets, the size of the sun in comparison with the other planets and other galactic information. The numbers and details help put into perspective our human day to day issues and the brevity of our lives as compared with the light years it can take for the light of a star to reach planet Earth.

The globe at the News Building rotates faster than the real Earth, returning to its original position within minutes, rather than 24 hours. But the inclination of the axis and the outlines of the continents are accurate and could be a great backdrop for a very entertaining geography or astronomy lesson.

Inlaid into the floor around the globe is a compass rose indicating the four cardinal points: north, east, west and south (the first letters of which spell the word news). Along the outer perimeter of the rose is a circular pathway in white marble with inlaid brass lines that point in the direction of major cities around the world. Next to the name of each city there is a number signifying the distance in miles between that city and the News Building.

Around the globe there are six plaques, each with a hypothetical situation involving a calculation regarding the size of the Earth, the sun and the moon and the distances between them and the stars. They state the following:

"If the sun were the size of this globe and placed here, the Earth would be the size of a walnut and located at the main entrance to Grand Central Terminal." (Grand Central Terminal is only three blocks away from the News Building.)

"If the sun were the size of this globe and placed here, then comparatively the Great Nebula in the constellation of Andromeda would be another globe one and a half billion miles in diameter, ten and a half billion miles away."

"If the sun were the size of this globe and placed here, then comparatively the moon would be one third of an inch in diameter and placed at the main entrance to Grand Central Station."

"If the sun were the size of this globe and placed here, then comparatively Alpha Centauri, the nearest fixed star, would be the size of the globe and would be 68,000 miles away (about two and a half times around the earth or a third of the distance to the moon)."

"If the sun were the size of this globe and placed here, then comparatively Arcturus, whose light was used to open the Chicago World Fair, would be another globe 324 feet in diameter 500,000 miles away." (The Chicago Fair, dedicated to a century of progress, was opened in 1933. The fair grounds were opened when the lights were automatically activated, as soon as light from the rays of the star Arcturus was detected.)

"If the sun were the size of this globe and placed here, then comparatively the Struve's star, the largest known, would be another globe seven miles in diameter placed 46 miles away." (This last plaque points to the age of the building which was completed in 1930. Struve's star is no longer considered to be the largest known star. The science of astronomy has made huge strides since the plaques were inserted in the lobby of the News Building.)

The News Building was originally named the Daily News Building because it was built to house the New York Daily News. The paper moved its headquarters to another location on 33rd Street in 1995. The Art-Deco skyscraper was designed by architect Raymond Hood who had also designed the Rockefeller Center.

The News Building was the model for the offices of the fictional Daily Planet newspaper, featured in the first two Superman movies. This is where Superman worked as the journalist Kent Clark alongside his colleague reporter Lois Lane, with whom he was romantically involved.

The lobby of the News Building also features photographs from outer space. The picture of the Earth rising over the lunar horizon, for example, was taken during the Apollo 8 mission in December 1968, which lasted for 147 hours. There is also a beautiful photograph of the Earth taken during the Apollo 13 mission in 1970 which was aborted after 56 hours due to the lack of pressure in the service module.

The lobby display also includes a mural of the solar system, which shows the paths taken by the Pioneer, Voyager and Mariner spacecrafts. Further exhibits include a picture of the first observed spiral galaxy, a clock which displays twelve time zones as well as weather instruments showing humidity, rainfall, atmospheric pressure and temperature, wind velocity and direction.

Perhaps less comprehensive than a visit to the planetarium or a science museum, yet the lobby of the News Building is a great place to better understand the relative distances between our galaxy and distant stars and to feel the humility that comes with an appreciation of our place in the universe.

I was looking around at the News Building display when suddenly I felt someone standing behind me. I turned abruptly and to my surprise came face to face with Richard Raven.

"I knew you would be here," he said.

"How did you know?" I didn't believe him. He shrugged his shoulders. "I just knew," he said. Then he added, "This building is one of my favorite places in all of New York. It helps put things into perspective, don't you think?"

I had to agree. "It certainly does," I said. "We are just a small speck of dust somewhere on the outer reaches of the Milky Way."

"Here today, gone tomorrow," he added. We stood there for a moment looking at the giant globe.

"How about lunch?" Richard said. He looked at his watch. "It's one o'clock," he added.

"All right," I said. "Where shall we go?"

"Let's go to the Oyster Bar," Richard replied. "It's located in the Grand Central Terminal, a few blocks away from here."

"Who are you?" I asked, once we had sat down and were given the menus. I was thinking of his business card which mentioned that he was a Merlin.

"A merlin is a bird," he said. "It is a rank and a station in a secret esoteric society."

"So how do you become a member if it is secret?" I asked.

"It evolves by word of mouth. When you are ready, you meet someone who tells you about it." He paused, then he looked at me intently. "I think you are ready. I think that is why we met." I blushed. "Ready for what?" I asked.

"Have you ever heard the saying, 'When the student is ready, the teacher will appear'?"

"Yes, I have," I confirmed. "I have had several teachers in my life," I added.

"Like who?"

"Well, there was my grandmother who was a healer. Then there is this strange mystery school that I keep dreaming about."

"Tell me about it," he said and I promptly recounted my recent nighttime adventures.

"It sounds to me like you've been astral traveling," he said.

"What's that?" I asked.

"Everybody has an astral body which lives in the blood. It is basically an energy body or double which can leave the physical body and travel to other places and other times. The energy body needs to be charged to be able to travel outside the physical body."

"Isn't that dangerous?" I asked.

"When you astral travel you are connected to your body by a silver thread so you will always return. Do you wake up freezing when you come back from these so-called dreams?"

"As a matter of fact, I do," I said as I recalled waking up shaking with cold.

"I love to astral travel. You can go to so many places absolutely free." I was not sure whether he was joking or not. Could he really have so much control over his astral adventures?

As if reading my mind, he added, "One needs to practice to be able to consciously astral travel at will. Maybe we could meet one day on the astral plane," he added. I just smiled and started eating my salad.

Chapter Ten

Justice

That night my astral travel dream reoccurred. I was back at the school and I was sitting at a table in the cafeteria, when suddenly I noticed two children playing on the steps leading from the terrace to the garden. It was a boy and a girl and they both looked to be about six years old. This was curious because I had never seen any children here before and I wondered whose they were. I had just finished breakfast and I decided to speak with them. I got up and approached them, and as I did so, I noticed that the little girl was holding an apple. The boy was holding out his hand, attempting to take the fruit away from her, and I heard the little girl saying, "Mommy said we should share it, so it's not yours; it belongs to both of us."

"But I want my share now," said the boy. "Let me bite my half."

"No, you'll bite too much," said the girl as she moved away from him further along the step and put her hand holding the apple behind her back.

"I think I can help," I said, as I approached the two children. "I'll bring a knife from my table and I'll cut the apple in half. That should be fair. What do you think?

"All right," said the boy, "but I get to choose which half."

"No, that's not fair," the little girl said. "Mommy always lets one of us cut and the other choose."

"Mm, that sounds fair," I said as I remembered that that was exactly how disputes were solved in my house when I was growing up with my younger brother, Steven. I got up and went over to the table I had just vacated. The cutlery was still there where I had left it, so I picked up a knife and a plate and brought them over to where the children were sitting on the step.

"All right then—here you are." I handed the knife to the girl. "If you cut the apple, then he can choose."

"All right," she said as she took the knife from me. She carefully placed the apple and the plate on the step and slowly attempted to cut the apple. The knife was a spreading knife and quite blunt, so at first it would not cut through the skin of the apple. I helped her by putting extra pressure on the knife, at the same time slightly readjusting the positioning of the blade, so that the result of the cutting would be more equal to two halves and thus more fair.

The boy hesitated for a moment, then reached for the piece that appeared to be slightly bigger and ran off, skipping down the path.

The little girl looked at me and took a bite from her part of the apple. With her mouth full, she mumbled "Thank you" and ran off following her brother.

I sat there for a moment, thinking about fairness and justice, until I saw the Master approach. Before I had time to rise, he sat down beside me on the step and started to speak, "Consider the two justices," he said. "There is human justice and then there is natural justice or planetary justice."

"What do you mean?" I enquired.

"Well, take the example of the two children sharing an apple." he replied. "Human justice would say that both children should get exactly half each. But that is an over-simplification and does not take into consideration all the facts. For example, one of the children might have a chemical deficiency that an apple would help to alleviate, whereas the other child could be perfectly robust and healthy without it. Or one child might be bigger than the other with a higher rate of metabolism and might require more

Justice

nourishment than the other. One child might even be allergic to apples and its system might reject its half. One of the children might hate the taste of apples altogether. There are so many considerations to take into account when looking for real justice, that it is quite simply beyond the human capability.

"The human justice system is an attempt at fairness, but we all know that it is faulty and with flaws, just as human perception is. Therefore the best place to look for justice is nature. Nature is harmonious, true and fair, though the human would not see it that way. In the natural worlds a lion eats a gazelle and a fox steals a chicken to survive. Neither have any morals or scruples about committing the act. Natural justice allows killing for survival. Some would say that nature is not fair, and this crops up when a good person falls ill or a child dies. But what they don't appreciate or know is the reason for these occurrences. We cannot know all the reasons why bad things happen. When humans were given choice, they were also given the responsibility for their actions, and their actions do have far-reaching consequences. We might not know what those consequences are, so although you might consider yourself to be fair and just, sometimes you are not. Don't you favor one friend over another? If you donate to charity, what is your reasoning for choosing one organization over another?"

I opened my mouth to answer, but he stopped me. "Don't answer that," he said. "I am just making a point. You are not on trial here."

Chapter Eleven

Alice in Wonderland

The next morning I received a call from Mrs. Grey. When I heard her voice, I was full of anticipation, in the hope that the job of assistant or even receptionist would be mine. But to my dismay she wanted to speak about something quite different.

"I got your number from your application," she said. "I am phoning you with a request. Please let this be in confidence between us."

"Sure," I replied, my curiosity now having been piqued. What is this about?"

Mrs. Grey hesitated for a moment. "When you shook my hand yesterday it felt like a bolt going straight into my chest. I haven't had any pain since and I have been breathing quite normally." She took a moment, as if she were checking her breathing. Then she spoke again, "I wonder if you could perform a healing on me?" she tentatively asked.

I was surprised. I had indeed been told before that I had healing hands and in the past I had participated in some healing sessions. In fact, my grandmother was a healer and after a series of sessions with her my own breast cancer was totally cured when I was in my early twenties. I also had had a friend who was a healer and I had learned from him about energy work and the laying on of hands. But never had I attempted to do such work myself. I hesitated.

"I am not sure I can..." I started to speak, but Mrs. Grey interrupted me.

"Please," she pleaded. "I don't care if you don't know what to do," she added, as if she were reading my thoughts. Just try. That's all I ask."

Another pause. From somewhere deep inside me a new confidence began to rise. "I can try, but with conditions," I said.

"Name your price," Mrs. Grey said, audibly relieved.

"No, I don't want your money," I replied. "And I will not call it healing. I don't want to claim I am something I am not. I will call it energy work. I will simply attempt to clear the energies around you that are blocked and if you get better, then it is not me but your own immune system doing the job."

"Yes, whatever you say," said Mrs Grey. "When can we start?"

"Come over tomorrow," I replied, sensing the urgency in her voice. I gave her the address and put the phone down. I felt scared on the one hand but I knew I needed to do this on the other. I had read a lot about faith healing, energy healing and various so-called miraculous cures. I believed it was possible. If others could do it, perhaps I could, too.

I felt I needed to think. I went outside and walked to Central Park. Somehow I ended up by the beautiful statue of Alice in Wonderland.

Alice in Wonderland has always been a favorite book of my childhood—full of mystery and esoteric knowledge. If you take the idea of growing to be large and then shrinking into diminutive proportions, this might not be possible physically, but energetically it certainly is. We can grow large or diminish in stature depending upon how we think of ourselves. A small person can be huge in stature, like a Napoleon or a Gandhi, and a big person can energetically be quite small.

In Central Park there is a bronze stature of Alice sitting on a toadstool, surrounded by some of the characters from the book. The Cheshire cat sits grinning nearby. Who has ever seen a cat disappear and his grin remaining? And yet, when we think of another person, we connect to their energy and usually it is their eyes and their words that we remember best, as we connect to another human through the energy emitted by their eyes and through their speech.

They say the eyes are the windows to the soul and indeed, it is the only living tissue that we see when we look at another person. It is through the eyes that we connect to their truth—the eyes don't lie. Words, on the other hand, can lie, but the energy concealed within them do not. Each letter, each word, as well as the pauses between the words and sentences carry a charge, which can be felt and deciphered by our instinct.

Lewis Carroll, who was a mathematician, was fascinated by language and he understood the power, beauty and intricacies of the English language, using words to convey humor, feelings and a sense of the absurd. The world he created in *Alice's Adventures in Wonderland* and *Through the Looking Glass* is a lasting contribution to our collective consciousness and an exercise in mind expanding acceptance of the ridiculous and the imaginative.

To me life's surprises have always verged on the improbable and I believe life's charm lies in its unpredictability, if only one can accept the constant changes and "go with the flow." Energetically we are creatures of change, altering our field all the time, like a chameleon, depending on our mood, our feelings, our thoughts, the weather, the time of day and the chores facing us at any particular time.

The Queen of Spades is always calling for our heads to be chopped off, while we are also receiving conflicting instructions from our own Cheshire cat. The only way out of this crazy world into sanity is to listen to our instinct and our inner guide which is prompted by the spirit. That is the only way out of our rabbit hole back into the sunlight.

When Alice asks the Cheshire cat which way she should go, he in turn asks her which way she would like to go. But when Alice admits she doesn't know, the Cheshire cat can't help her.

It's like that with us and the energy worlds or the spirit worlds or the angelic realms. If we don't know what we want and are not able to express our desires in words, we cannot be helped. How can we achieve our dreams if we don't know what they are?

In·sight: MOMENTS OF BEING

So it is best to start somewhere, anywhere and decide what you want to achieve. It can be something small, like a short term goal that is easily achievable. Then once that first step is accomplished, perhaps the next goal post will reveal itself. Just don't drift like a piece of driftwood in the ocean, but choose a direction, any direction, otherwise you might as well be running around in circles.

As I stood contemplating the charm of Alice in Wonderland and the immortal characters Lewis Carroll had created, a group of children approached the statue. There was a guide with them who obviously knew a lot about the book and the meaning behind the many references introduced by the author.

"It is a well known fact that Lewis Carroll was a mathematician. But he was also a gifted photographer with a profound love of language and logic," the guide said.

"His real name was Charles Dodgson and he taught mathematics at Christ Church College at Oxford University. He was one of the scientists who were concerned about the fact that at the time it was unclear where on the planet the date should change so that a person traveling around the world could plan his or her itinerary according to universally established schedules for boats and trains. The International Date Line was put in place in 1884. It mainly goes through uninhabited territory covered by the Pacific Ocean, and it bends east or west to avoid such land masses as the archipelago of Tonga or Fiji. It mostly runs along the meridian of 180 degrees longitude. So if you were on a ship passing through the International Date Line there could be two dates occurring at the same time on that vessel. You could be standing with one foot in Friday and the other in Saturday, for example.

"The books *Alice's Adventures in Wonderland* and *Through the Looking Glass* have many examples where language is used according to how it sounds or the double meaning of words is employed, adding curious twists and references to the conversation. Some of the dialogue is best read out loud to get full value from the hidden meanings of the language.

"For example, when the Mock Turtle tells his story, he mentions that the master who had taught him was called Tortoise by the students. A reader might not notice, but when telling the story out loud, it becomes obvious that the name Tortoise sounds very similar to the words *taught us*. The Mock Turtle further explains that he was taught reeling and writhing, rather than reading and writing, which is what human children, including Alice, were (and still are) taught at school.

"Who makes shoes under the sea? Soles and eels, of course. No doubt they specialize in soles and heals. Instead of blacking which was used in Alice's days to blacken shoes, the sea shoes were whitened with whitings. And so it continues—wise fish always have a porpoise, just as wise humans are meant to have a purpose.

"In *Through the Looking Glass* there are further examples of Dodgson's witty use of language. The talking flowers, for example, explain to Alice how they are protected by a tree. And how can that be? asks Alice. Because it could bark if any danger threatened them. A tree could say bough-wough with their boughs which sounds remarkably like a dog's bow-wow.

"And why don't we humans know that flowers can talk? Because most flower beds are too soft, so the flowers are always asleep and do not speak.

"Then there is the scene in the train when the horse speaks in a hoarse voice. The gnat then shows Alice the mysterious insects: the rocking-horse-fly, the snap-dragon-fly and the bread-and-butter-fly.

"Syllogism is a logical construct. The most famous syllogism, introduced by Aristotle states that if all men are mortal and all Greeks are men, therefore all Greeks are mortal. Dodgson turns the syllogism around into what he calls a sillygism. One such illogical construct could be the statement by the dormouse during the Mad Hatter's tea party, when he asks, waking from deep sleep, whether the fact that he breathes when he sleeps means that he sleeps when he breathes.

"Another example of Dodgson's wit is when Alice tells the White King she saw nobody in the woods and he admires her acute eyesight, to be able to see Nobody at a great distance.

In·sight: MOMENTS OF BEING

"It is hard to imagine a world without Alice's adventures and the many idioms and rhymes that have come into daily use from these classic stories," the guide completed his explanation and the group moved away, no doubt to look at one of the other special sites in Central Park.

I carried on looking at the statue. I felt like I had met my Cheshire cat. I needed to decide where I was going and what I wanted to be in my life. If I wanted to be a healer and a teacher, then I needed to tell my inner guide that that was what I wanted. I felt a resolve and decided there and then that I would do my best to perform a healing on Mrs. Grey and that I would try to help her. Something inside was nudging me forward and although I needed to earn a living, I felt that working for a corporation was not for me in the long term.

As I kept looking at the Cheshire cat, wondering what my purpose was, I swear I could see the cat smiling enigmatically at me. "Which way do you want to go?" he seemed to be asking.

"I want to be a teacher and a healer. I want to pass on to others everything I know." I realized I had said this out loud because a couple of heads turned and a parent who was standing nearby grabbed her young daughter by the hand and hurried away.

The Cheshire cat, though, was still there and looked very real.

"Then you must be faithful to your desire and work to make it so," the Cheshire cat said. I felt at that moment that my life had taken on a definite direction and a defined purpose.

Chapter Twelve

Belief

That night I had another vision, which I now understood to be an astral travel dream. I was sitting in the library of the mystery school, reading a book about fairies, when a young girl approached me and asked whether she could join me. She obviously badly wanted some company, because she could clearly see that I was fully engaged in my reading, and yet she was able to voice her request.

"Please, sit down," I said, as I picked up the book mark that was lying on the table in front of me, marked my place and closed the book. I noticed that I had placed it on my lap, rather than on the table, subconsciously indicating that I intended to return to it soon.

"What are you reading?" the girl asked, as she cocked her head, trying to read the title that was sideways to her line of vision at a ninety degree angle.

"Oh, just a story about fairies," I said, attempting to sound casual, in case she thought that I was not a serious reader, prone to reading fairy tales for children and New Age books about angels and dragons and the like. Why I should have been bothered or preoccupied with what she might think of me escapes me now. I can no longer think why I should have cared.

All this was going through my head. Clearly my stay at the school was making me more aware of my thoughts and actions. Not necessarily more refined or developed, just more aware.

"Do you believe in fairies?" she asked. She had red hair that fell to her shoulders in frizzy waves, a lot of freckles on her upturned nose and bright, penetrating, inquisitive, very green eyes.

"No, I don't." I shrugged my shoulders and smiled, almost apologetically. "I've never seen one," I added, as an afterthought.

"So, you only believe in what you see?" It was more a question than a challenge.

"Well, it's easier to believe, if you see something. After all, they do say that seeing is believing."

"Well, what about the air then? You don't see the air, do you?"

"No, I don't. But I can feel it as it fills my lungs." I took a deep breath, to demonstrate my point.

"And what about electricity in that wire?" She pointed to the wire leading from a lamp to the socket in the wall. "What about that? You haven't seen an electrical current, have you?"

"No, but I have seen its results. I have seen a light bulb light up and I have even received a shock from putting my finger into the socket when there was no bulb there, but the lamp was on."

"So you only believe what you see and what you feel? Is that it?"

This was becoming uncomfortable. Why was she challenging me? I did not want to sound defensive, so I thought for a while before I responded.

"No," I said slowly. "There are other things I believe in." I took a moment to think. "I believe in the power of love."

Oh God, that sounded so banal, so I quickly added, "And I believe in an unseen energy that some people might call God."

"You know as well as I do that there is power and energy in everything. I believe that fairies, just like angels or nature spirits or entities are conglomerates of energy that acquire a form and can become visible within the human range."

"So have you seen one? A fairy, I mean?" I asked.

"Yes, as a matter of fact, I have. But I think that the only reason I did was because I believed that they existed. I was a young girl of nine or ten, playing with my sister in the garden. We had built a house for fairies out of twigs and leaves, with acorns as stools and decorated it with flowers and colorful berries. The next day when we came to look at our construction, a little fairy flew out of our little house and escaped into the bushes a few yards away. She didn't look exactly like the drawings in your book, not like a little lady with a wand, but she did have wings. She looked more like a dragonfly than a picture book fairy."

"Then how did you know she was a fairy and not a dragonfly?"

"Because she was see-through and she glowed with a million sparkles coming off her. We both saw her and we both were certain at the time that we had seen a fairy. And there was something else."

"What's that?' I leaned forward with interest.

"She seemed to communicate to both of us as she flew away."

"What? What did she say?" I was really intrigued now.

"It wasn't as if she said anything. It was more that we both understood that she was grateful for her little house. She somehow also communicated to us that she would be leaving now and that she would no longer need the shelter we had so generously provided. We both received the same words at the same time, though not a sound was heard. How could we doubt it?"

"That's amazing." I said. "Did you ever see her again?" I then asked.

"No, that was the only time. We used to check out the garden regularly, but we never saw anything like it again. And then we grew up and forgot about the whole thing."

"Well, I do wish I could have an experience like that."

"But you can. I think the only reason we were able to see a fairy that day is because we believed in their existence. Perhaps the old saying should be reversed to 'believing is seeing.'"

I thanked her for her insight and as she got up to leave, I re-opened my book with renewed interest.

Chapter Thirteen

The Cloisters

The next day Mrs. Grey came over to the apartment. At first I sat down with her and explained that I was not claiming to do anything or be anything but that I would attempt to clear any energetic blockages I might find in her aura. I would not touch her unless she would give me clear permission to do so. She told me that since our encounter two days earlier she had not experienced any pain and her breathing seemed unobstructed and flowing with ease.

I asked her to lay down on the sofa and at first I simply raised my hand over her chest and held it there for a few moments. I felt heat, almost a burning sensation in my right hand. That was strange because I was holding my hand at least two feet above her body. Following my instinct I gathered up the heat as if it were a piece of fluff and flicked it away. I did this several times and as I did so I saw that Mrs. Grey was relaxing and breathing deeper. Her eyes were closed and within minutes she had fallen asleep. I continued using my right hand to clear away the energy that had gathered in front of the woman's chest. When I felt that the heat was gone and the temperature had dropped, I paused.

"Mrs. Grey," I said, but she did not answer. She was deeply asleep. I picked up a blanket and covered her up. I then went into the kitchen to put the kettle on.

Mrs. Grey slept for over half an hour. When she finally woke up she was disorientated. The first words out of her mouth were, "What time is it?"

"A quarter past four," I replied. "You've been sleeping for a while," I said.

She sat up. "I must be going. It's late. I need to get back. Thank you for seeing me," she said at the door. "I'll call you."

"Okay. Take it easy. You are in a very relaxed state. Try not to hurry."

"It's true," she confirmed. "I feel like I've been sleeping for a week. Thank you. Are you sure I cannot pay you for your time?"

"No, that's absolutely fine," I said. "I am not a professional. I have no qualifications."

"I don't think there are any qualifications for what you were doing. I think this is a new science. I know all about alternative therapies, but this was different. It was as if it was powered by a different kind of energy."

"I think you are right about that. I felt it too. But we need to find out a lot more about it before there is an official qualification. Who knows whether mainstream medicine will ever embrace energy work?"

"I understand some hospitals already do. There are nurses who practice Therapeutic Touch. They have some great results. But of course there are also doctors and hospitals who claim it is all nonsense," Mrs. Grey said.

"Well, they will have to change their mindset," I replied. "The energy of the planet is changing. People are becoming interested in energy healing. They are beginning to see colors around people. They are seeing the energy of an aura. Where was Reiki thirty years ago? But now thousands subscribe to it."

"That is very reassuring. This planet could do with a major overhaul." Mrs. Grey smiled as I handed her her coat and opened the door.

"Let me know how you feel tomorrow," I said.

"I'll call," she replied as she turned away and walked down the stairs.

After she had left I felt there was still an energetic residue of her sickness in the room. I thoroughly cleaned the room and lit some incense.

The Cloisters

I also rang a bell and opened a window, and finally felt that the atmosphere in the room had cleared.

The next morning I visited the Cloisters. I figured that if I wanted to see more of New York, I would need to do it now, before I started working. I had heard about the Cloisters and the gardens, located on a hill above the Hudson River and wanted to see the site where Fort Washington was gallantly defended in 1776 during the war for independence by the Maryland and Virginia regiment. After its capture it was named Fort Tryon in honor of the last English governor of New York, William Tryon (1729-1788).

At the Cloisters I found the multiple relics and styles, brought from all over Europe, confusing. The best part is the cloisters themselves—the columned covered walkway around a central courtyard—where the meditative atmosphere of perambulation lodged there by centuries of monks attending to their religious duties still prevails.

The reliquaries in the shape of human heads that used to contain bone fragments of saints or splinters of crosses or other memorabilia of objects that holy men and women had touched and imbued with their energy and frequency gave me food for thought. As in Cologne Cathedral in Germany, reliquaries were often the centerpiece of a medieval church or cathedral. It was believed that the bones of saints maintained their energy long after the person's demise, radiating their saintly qualities into the congregation. Although the composition of a person's DNA might have been unknown in ancient times, the power of a strand of hair or an object that had belonged to a saintly person and was used on a repetitive basis throughout their life was well understood. A knight would go into battle, or into a tournament, or ride off into the distance on a knightly quest wearing a token he had received from his lady. Many romantic ladies would wear a lock of hair of their beloved, thus connecting to his energy and frequency during a prolonged absence abroad or at war defending his country. Love letters tied together with a ribbon are reminders of past intimacy and carry a charge that can bring back sweet memories of a past affair. Houses and buildings are depositories of their history and although most people are no longer sensitive enough to connect to the colorful past deposited in metal and stone, there are many stories of people unexpectedly catching a glimpse from history through the veil of time. In his book, *Memories, Dreams, Reflections* Carl Jung, for example, tells the story of admiring a series of paintings in a historic building, later learning that these paintings had been removed from the site many years before his visit.

When something dramatic happens, like a murder or a battle, the energetic imprint is so powerful that it can often be seen and felt by people for generations afterwards. The attack on Fort Erie by British soldiers in 1812, for example, left such a scar on the atmosphere of the place that even recently unexplained shadows and words like "horrible" and "kill" were recorded on tape by a crew of ghost seekers.

Haunted houses, castles and palaces remain energetically disturbed until the event that had caused the haunting can be somehow counterbalanced and its remaining energy dissipated. It might take years for this to happen. Likewise, our personal energy field, known as the aura, can also be haunted by past trauma and events until we are able to find reconciliation, forgiveness and peace.

These thoughts came to me while walking around the Cloisters and sensing the atmospheres and energies imbued in the walls, furniture, paintings, windows and wall hangings that have been placed there. At one point I thought I could see a monk walking underneath the cloister arches surrounding a small herbal garden. His hands were folded into his habit, and he looked like he was in contemplation or prayer. As he passed by me, I could tell he was not a real person, but some kind of energy formation, chimera or ghost. However, he did communicate to me telepathically and this is what he said: "There are major changes coming to your world. The Earth needs to be healed and people need healing, too. There are those among you who were born with a specific purpose—to heal, teach and help others. You are one of them."

As he passed by and continued walking, the image slowly disintegrated into a mist and then completely disappeared.

Chapter Fourteen

Humility

That night I had yet another dream about the mysterious Master who was my teacher. In my dream I got up early, as I had been instructed to go and see the Master before breakfast. I found him in the garden, walking along the path that led to a small pond, with his hands behind his back, obviously deep in thought.

As soon as I approached, he looked up and stopped in his tracks. "Greetings," he said. "Yes. I wanted to speak with you. I have a koan for you." When he saw my look of surprise and non-comprehension, he smiled and explained, "In Buddhist Zen tradition a koan is a riddle or a question which a neophyte meditates upon and comes up with an answer. The answer then tells the master what level of development the student has achieved. There is never one final answer or understanding that can be achieved; it is not like a test. What counts is the process itself and the effort to get there.

"However, as we are not Buddhists, there is no need to meditate in the lotus position; it would only cause you pain and discomfort, even if you were able to make your legs bend into the required configuration. You were brought up in the west and your muscles and bones have not been trained to sit cross-legged on a mat for long periods of time. You can therefore meditate as you go about your duties. When you eat your meals,

In·sight: MOMENTS OF BEING

drive a car and spend time with your friends—you can meditate any time, anywhere, as long as there is enough quiet from the outside and enough stillness inside."

The Master started walking again and I walked with him, waiting to hear the koan or riddle.

"I will give you a western koan to think about," he said, "and this will be your next tasking. The question I want you to answer is, 'If you were an angel, what would be the first thing you would attempt to do when arriving on planet Earth?'"

I sensed that this was the totality of my instructions, but before I went off to my duties, I had one more question, "How long have I got?" I asked.

"Let's say until tomorrow morning. That gives you twenty-four hours of meditation time." He hesitated for a moment, and then added with a smile, "Providing, of course, that you remember to meditate while you are engaged in other activities. We do not impose discipline as they do in Buddhist temples, but we do expect results." There was another moment of silence, during which I wondered what kind of results he was looking for. As if anticipating my thought process, he added, "And by results I do not mean the right answer. The result, as in a Zen temple, is the effect that the process will have upon you."

I sensed that the conversation was over, so I nodded my head to indicate I understood the instructions and quietly walked away.

After breakfast I went for a walk. There was a gentle breeze that brought with it a flowery fragrance from the garden. I walked toward the pond and sat down on a bench.

If I were an angel? How could I possibly know what an angel would do? Well, what did I know about angels? It would seem, from the scriptures I had read, that angels are concerned with human welfare; they protect and serve. They are the messengers of God, bringing tidings and prophecies of significant events in human history. Thus, if I were an angel, I would have these concerns as my priority. I would know about the future, so I would be able to predict what was to come. I would look for the righteous people

Humility

on this planet and ask them to help me work for the survival of the human race. I would appear to the important people in the world and guide them in their decisions toward peace and prosperity. I would warn people about oncoming disasters and tell them what to do to be saved. I would be a beacon of hope in dark times and a reminder of the human quest in good times. I would work tirelessly for the survival of the human race!

I had been lost in thought for a long time, and suddenly I realized that the sun was rising higher in the sky and that I had been sitting for hours in one place, totally absorbed in my own thoughts. How curious that I needed a prompt from outside to become interested in my own thought processes! I got up from the bench and started walking toward the main building.

The rest of the day passed in much the same vein. Whatever I did and wherever I went—in the building, in the dining room, in the bedroom, walking the grounds—and whoever I spoke to, there was a constant background wondering and wonderment about what it would be like to be an angel.

One thing I realized was the pain an angel must feel when considering the state of the world and the various conflicts that always seem to be taking place somewhere around the globe. It made me think about religious wars in times gone by and the various crimes people have committed in the name of their beliefs and their religion. Human behavior must cause much grief to an angel.

I stayed up late that night, writing a petition to an angel, asking for guidance. Finally, I went to bed tired and worried, concerned that I had not yet come up with an adequate answer to the koan, even though I knew that getting it right was not the object of the exercise.

The next morning came very quickly, or so it seemed, and I was soon on my way to the interview room where I was supposed to meet with the Master. I knocked on the door and walked in. The Master was waiting, looking expectant. He did not need to ask. I sat down and started to speak, "I cannot know what an angel would do because I do not know how an angel thinks. It would seem that angels know about the future and are able to predict it and warn people about what is going to happen. If I knew what was going to occur, I could help people survive natural and unnatural disasters, I could let them know when a new prophet would be born...; I would be a messenger and a rescuer. My main purpose and concern would be the survival and evolutionary upgrade of the human race."

I paused for a moment. I seemed to run out of things to say. The Master waited for a moment and when there was still silence between us, he commented, "The idea of the koan is not to get the right answer. It is a way of thinking and a process that can help you in your understanding or demonstrate to you your lack of understanding; it can help you in your development. The fact that you thought about it is everything; it took you away from your preoccupation with self into the domain of being with an intelligence that is greater than human. It made you wonder what it would be like to have the power of clairvoyance and prophecy. The exercise brought you into the realms of what a human would call the supernatural, but really should be called natural because it is just that—an angel is an embodiment of a natural power. It is an angle of approach that universal energy can take to reach this planet and sometimes even appear to humans in visible form. There are numerous stories of angels being seen over battlefields or helping out in distress; or, as in the biblical story, they are known to bring tidings of joy and blessings.

"The exercise made you at least attempt to think like an angel. This is not out of your reach, but it will take a lot of practice and a lot of belief. It will help you develop a global view and concerns that are larger than your own."

He paused for a moment and then spoke again. "You have done well and I think you have experienced the essence of humility, as you realized that there are beings that know more than we do and have the abilities and skills that we long for. Remember this experience and you will be able to feel the essence of humility again and again, for without it you would never be able to see reality from outside your own limited field of vision."

Humility

And with that he nodded in a way that told me that this interview was over and I needed to be on my way.

Chapter Fifteen

The Garden of Stones

I have always thought I was special. I also thought that everyone else thought they were special, too. But when I had asked a girl at school whether she thought she was special, to my surprise she said no, she didn't think so.

I still think I am special and I think that everyone in the world is special, too. Everyone has a special talent that is unique to them, even if they are not aware of it or haven't discovered it yet. I believe it is there to be developed and fostered over time. My special talent is that I am clairvoyant and I am sensitive to the energy realms of the planet. I see what others cannot see and hear a whole range of voices that to others are silent.

When I got up in the morning I was still thinking about my mysterious encounter with the monk at the Cloisters the day before. I also remembered my dream and wondered about the angelic influence in my life and in the lives of others. I could think of times when I had been guided and helped, as if an invisible intelligence was with me, gently pointing the way. I had two more interviews lined up for the following week and I thought I should do some research about the two companies before going there. Just as I was about to start my search and had booted up the computer, the telephone rang. It was Mrs. Grey—she was calling, just as she had promised she would.

"You had asked me to let you know how I felt yesterday," she said. "I felt very relaxed after the healing and today I am feeling a lot better. Yesterday was almost as if I was drunk or something."

"That's the energy," I said. "It has that effect on people. It's intoxicating. It won't last, but even as it wears off you should feel better than before."

"I am seeing the doctor in a few days," she said. I will be interested to see what he has to say."

"Let me know," I said.

"I have good news for you," Mrs. Grey then said. "I have been authorized to offer you a job."

Now I really got excited. I waited to hear what she had to say next. "We are offering you the job of assistant to the PR department. You will start off by helping me out organizing advertising campaigns. There will also be some work helping the warehouse managers, organizing deliveries and dealing with clients—just the kind of work you used to do. Then when I leave, you would be working with whoever takes over my position." She then proceeded to explain the details—the salary, the hours (which were to be flexible), the forms I would need to fill out and the agreement I would need to sign. "You can start Monday," she said.

"That's great," I replied.

As soon as I put the phone down, it rang again. It was Richard. He wanted to meet. "Come to the second floor café at the Museum of Jewish Heritage," he said. "I have something to show you." Intrigued, I agreed.

The Museum of Jewish Heritage is located in a beautiful building in Lower Manhattan, situated on the bank of the Hudson River. It is a living memorial to those who perished in the Holocaust. The building itself, designed by Kevin Roche, John Dinkeloo and Associates is topped by a pyramid—a six-sided structure which is called the Living Memorial to the Holocaust. It was established in 1997 and still has that feeling of newness, although the exhibits are permeated with memories of the tragedy inflicted on the Jewish people during the Second World War.

When I went up to the second floor, I saw that Richard was standing

The Garden of Stones

inside the café by the glass doors leading onto a terrace overlooking the Hudson River and the Statue of Liberty in the distance.

"Look at that," he said and I stood there spellbound. I was looking at a series of huge boulders, each one with an indentation carved out of the top of it, within which miniature trees had been planted.

"That is amazing," I said. "What is it?"

"It's called *The Garden of Stones* and it was designed by a Scottish artist, Andy Goldsworthy," he explained. "Known for his work with the natural elements, Andy has put together a remarkable display in honor of the victims of the Holocaust and its survivors.

"As you can see, *The Garden of Stones* consists of 18 boulders that were chosen by the artist during his search through the northeastern states. He found what he was looking for in Barre, Vermont. The size and weight of the stones vary—the lightest weighs three tons; the heaviest 13.

"Once Andy found the boulders, he hollowed each one using various methods: either burning the indentation out with a flame torch, cutting them into the stone with a water jet or by coring. He then planted a dwarf oak tree in each stone. The trees have been growing from the stones since the exhibit was first opened in 2003. They have grown over the years and the stones and the plants have become intertwined in a mutual destiny. They are expected to grow to become 12 feet tall, but in the meantime visitors can watch their growth pattern as each stage of growth has been documented in a photographic record."

"Why are there 18?" I asked.

"Each letter of the Hebrew alphabet has a numeric value," Richard continued. "The number for the letter *Chai* is 18 and *Chai* means life. The trees were planted by Holocaust survivors, their families and the artist himself. As time passes, this memorial exhibit is a testimony to the partnership of the hard and the soft, the transient and the enduring, the struggle and the stillness."

"Can we go out?" I asked.

"Yes, we can." He opened the door and we stepped out onto the terrace.

The boulders were set on a bed of sand and it felt like walking out into nature. In the distance I could see the Statue of Liberty.

"I feel this is a contemplative space where one can meditate about the history of the human race, the atrocities of the Holocaust and the strength of the human spirit," I said.

"Yes," Richard confirmed. "This space is dedicated to those who perished within the Holocaust and those who survived. It is an exposé to the indomitability of hope and survival. That is why I love coming here. It gives me hope."

We fell silent for a moment. I got the feeling this would become a favorite haunt of mine, too, where I could meditate in peace, overlooking the Hudson River and the Statue of Liberty.

When I got back to the apartment I looked up Andy Goldsworthy on line and found out that his art consists of natural ingredients, often combining such elements as stones, twigs, flowers, flowing water, ice and light. Featured in the documentary *Rivers and Tides* by Thomas Riessheimer, Andy would walk through the British landscape close to his home where he responded to the various elements he would find. He composed images that are not only beautiful, but play on the senses and evoke inklings of other dimensions.

For example, in the movie he shapes wands of ice by warming the frozen liquid in his hands, then suspends the latticework from a bush and waits until the setting sun shines through the ice creating a dance of light and shadows. He takes a picture of the illuminated icy filigree and then the moment is gone as the sun sets; only a photograph remains. Or he weaves some fallen branches together and suspends the latticework from a tree, forming an empty circle surrounded by twigs. It creates the sense that there is something there behind the empty space, like a gateway to another world.

I felt that I was catching glimpses of another world through my experiences of the past few days. The Master I was dreaming about since arriving in New York, the monk I saw at the Cloisters, Joan of Arc's voices and even the Cheshire cat from *Alice in Wonderland* were all indicators that there is more to life than meets the eye. This is why I felt it was so important to open one's heart and intuition to the possibility of unseen friends and to the fact that we do have more senses than the five that are given to us at birth to deal with the material worlds.

Chapter Sixteen

Service

That night the dream reoccurred. This time I dreamed that I had awoken from sleep and I had received a message to go and see the Master early in the morning, before breakfast. The little room at the back of the building was called the Round Room as it was located in a round turret, perhaps added on after the original construction was completed. I knocked on the door and heard a gentle call.

"Come in." The Master was sitting at a small round table and there was a chair placed on the other side, facing him.

"Please, sit down." I did so and as soon as our eyes met, I began to relax. I realized at that moment that having been summoned to see him, I had reactivated a series of connotations connected with being called to the principal's office or the teachers' room. Here I knew there was nothing to fear but everything to win.

"It is time for you to learn about service," he said and I waited for more information, because I had no idea what he meant. "The tasking is simple," he added. "I want you to spend the day in the dining room, serving the three daily meals—breakfast, lunch and dinner. Take the opportunity of this tasking to observe yourself—your feelings, your thoughts and your responses. I will see you back here later tonight when the work is done. You can then tell me what you have learned."

It took a moment to absorb what he was saying. Finally, I asked, "Who should I report to?"

"After we've finished, go and see Rose, the head waitress. She will tell you what to do."

I could feel the disappointment rising in me; after all, I had come here to learn, not to work. But by now I had also learned to trust the Master and I wasn't going to show my feelings. However, he seemed to sense that something was amiss.

"Are you clear with my instructions?" he asked.

"Yes, I am," I replied. "I'll be on my way." I stood up and took one final look at him. He smiled and the warmth of his smile made me feel better. As if answering my thoughts, he said, "You are here to learn about yourself and about life and about the promise of human development. There are many ways to learn; in fact, everything is a lesson—from the moment you wake up in the morning until you go to bed at night. If serving meals can teach you about life, then serving meals is a progressive thing to do. Everyone here helps out with the many chores. The only employed staff here are Mary the cook, Rose the head waitress, the cleaner, my secretary and the head gardener who doubles up as a driver. We also have a book-keeper who comes in once a month and we employ a company to do the laundry, and that is it. If there were more people employed, you probably could not have been able to afford the course. So please cooperate in good faith and try to learn something useful today."

I felt chastised and a bit ashamed of myself.

"I will see you tonight," he said as I turned around and walked toward the door.

As I entered the kitchen, I immediately understood that Mary the cook was queen and empress of this particular domain. It seemed that she was doing many things at once—looking into pots, stirring a number of brews, serving food onto plates and issuing commands to her single helper, a young girl in her twenties with blond hair escaping from underneath the white scarf that covered her head.

Service

"Are you Rose's helper today?" Mary asked as she continued to cut a cucumber and as the blond girl scooped up the pieces into a large bowl, which contained a salad, clearly being made ready for lunch. I nodded in confirmation and she immediately continued, waving the knife in the air as she did so, "Well, don't just stand there," she said. "Rose isn't here yet, so why don't you put on an apron..."—she indicated with her head a series of hooks with an assortment of white and not-so-white aprons on the wall next to the door to the dining room, "...and start serving. There's porridge in the green pot and scrambled eggs in the food warmer. Everything else is laid out for them in the dining room, but check the juice containers, and you might need to cut some extra pieces of bread."

I took an apron that appeared to be clean and crispy white off the hook and put it on. I then proceeded into the dining room to check supplies and take orders. I had never worked as a waitress before but somehow I seemed to know what to do. It was not busy in the dining room to begin with, but as time went on, more and more people began to appear.

I quite enjoyed the experience, perhaps because I knew I was only playing a part for a day. Tomorrow I would be sitting at a table in the dining room and someone else would be serving me.

However, by the time dinnertime came around, I was tired and my legs hurt. I wanted it to be over. I had had two short breaks during which I ate my meals after everyone else had finished theirs. As I sat at a small table, set up in the corner of the large kitchen and as I watched Mary the cook bustling around, opening fridges (of which there were two very large ones), cutting, grating, blending, cooking, baking, almost without a break, issuing commands to her assistant, I pondered about service. I was in service to those who came to eat, carrying plates of food out from the kitchen into the dining room; I was there to see they were well fed and that they had everything they needed. I shared a brief chat here, a smile there, trying to keep up with the various requests that were coming my way.

So what did I now feel about being in service? I felt both tired and satisfied. It seemed to me that service was akin to giving—it meant sharing one's time and energies with others, providing the necessities of life and, in this case, being an intermediary between the production line (i.e. the kitchen) and the consumers.

When the dinner guests had retired and at last Rose told me that I could hang up my apron back onto the hook next to the kitchen door, and the young girl whose name was Audrey was washing up the last dishes, I felt ready to go back to the Round Room and share my experiences of the day with the Master.

I knocked and went in, and he was sitting exactly where I had left him earlier that morning, as if he had been there all day. He looked up at me and I sat down in the chair opposite.

He continued to watch me and finally he asked after a pause, "So what have you discovered about service today?"

"It is very satisfying," I replied slowly and deliberately. He nodded and I continued, "At first I felt disgruntled because I felt I was being used. People saw me as a tool, a fetch-it machine, rather than a person." I was trying to be as honest as possible. "But then I settled to the fact that I was performing a function and I didn't mind any more. I was beginning to feel useful and that brought with it a certain satisfaction."

I hesitated for a moment and then added, "There were moments when I enjoyed the process of service and I felt that I was learning a new skill. But I do feel tired now. I think I have given all the energy I had to give."

He smiled and replied, "Then you have not connected to the real essence of service. When you do, you will be able to give of yourself in virtually inexhaustible quantities and for a very long time. Service is like a fountain that never runs out. But realize that the essence of service will not come to live with you just because you do things for others. Real service comes from the reasons why you do it. You started the day by doing it for me and that was not productive, because your will was being influenced from someone outside of yourself. Then you did it for everyone else which made you feel virtuous and gave you a certain satisfaction. Finally, you began to do it for you which caused you to be more engaged in what you were doing,

Service

but also brought with it an exhaustion, as you had used up your supply of energy, but failed to connect to a new and plentiful source. You could have taken the next step and performed your service for a more powerful reason. If you had done it because you wanted to facilitate the learning process of those who are here so they can become better human beings, then you could have plugged yourself into the source of reasoning that is in pursuit of human excellence. Now that is a very powerful motive and it brings with it endurance, resilience and a fine energy that can weather the demands of an unfamiliar task or a difficult understanding. If you ever feel tired when you are doing something, you need to ask yourself the question, 'Why am I doing this?' and if you cannot find a valid and satisfying reason, perhaps you should not be doing it. At this stage of your education, the fact that someone had asked you to do it is no longer a valid reason in itself."

We sat in silence for a moment as I pondered his words. "In that case any action can become productive and rewarding, providing it is thought through within the context of one's chosen path," I finally said in response.

"That is correct. For a person without an aim, it does not matter what they do. But once you have a purpose in your life, make sure that nothing takes you away from your chosen journey; even a little act or word or gesture can help you on your way, providing it is done for a valid reason. This is the difference between a haphazard and a deliberate life—it is up to you to decide which one you want to become."

With those words I could feel that the interview was over, for only I could decide who and what I wanted to be and why. I had much to think about, so I thanked the Master and quietly left the room.

Chapter Seventeen

Grand Central Terminal

The day I started work at The Healthy Gourmet I was introduced to the entire staff of the PR Department. They were in the process of preparing a new brochure, which was supposed to be ready for Thanksgiving. Everyone seemed somewhat tense and under pressure. The only person who acted relaxed and seemed to take it all in her stride was Mrs. Grey.

After the introductions she invited me into her office. Once she sat down behind her desk and I took the visitor's seat in front of her, she explained, "I want you to be the liaison between the PR Department and our customers. Make sure you respond promptly to requests for advertising materials or display boards. You will be dealing with stores all over the country—in New Jersey, California, Texas and Wyoming. Keep in touch with the warehouse managers there and make sure they have what they need. You will sometimes need to chase our suppliers and make sure orders are fulfilled promptly." She handed me a list of suppliers—it was several pages long. "Don't worry," she reassured me. "It will take you time to get to know these people and where they are located. It took me about six months."

"Does that mean you are leaving?" I asked.

"Not yet," Mrs. Grey said. "I feel so much better after that healing with you, I am no longer sure I will have to leave at all."

"Have you seen a doctor?" I asked. "What are they saying about your condition?"

"No, I haven't," Mrs. Grey replied. "I am going tomorrow. In the meantime, have a good look at our website and ordering procedure." She opened the drawer of her desk. "Here is your e-mail address and log in password. You can change it if you wish." She handed me a slip of paper with an e-mail address on it. "Check it out because I haven't looked at it yet, and there are bound to be unfulfilled orders in your mailbox. Pass them on to the relevant warehouses. We haven't been able to automate that step in the process, but we are working on it. At least it gives us some central control and the buyers can enjoy a person-to-person contact. You might also find a request from one of the warehouses in your in box. See if you can help them. Use your initiative." She smiled. I already felt overwhelmed, but tried hard not to show it.

"Where do you want me to sit?" I asked.

She stood up and came around to the front of the desk. "There is a small office next door," she said. "My secretary sits there and there is another desk in there which will be yours." I stood up and she led the way through a side door.

The next door office was indeed small and contained two desks. Behind the one nearest the door sat a young girl with dark hair and very dark lipstick.

"This is Elaine," Mrs. Grey said. I extended my arm and we shook hands. "Hi, my name is Barbara," I said.

"Elaine is my secretary. She can help you. She knows everyone in this office."

Mrs. Grey then walked over to the empty desk. "This will be your desk," she said. "The computer is a bit old but it will do for now. We'll get you a new one soon. Start by checking out the website and making a note of any suggestions you might have for improvement. Then check your e-mails and go through the list of suppliers I gave you. You might want to check out their websites as well so you know who and what you are dealing with. That should give you plenty to get on with." I walked behind the desk and put my bag in the bottom drawer of the pedestal. Mrs. Grey turned to go back to her office, but she then obviously had second thoughts because she returned and stood in front of what was now my desk. She bent over the desk and whispered in my ear so Elaine couldn't hear. "Come into my office," she said.

I followed her through the door to her office. She closed the door behind us. "I have a request," she said. It was curious how she suddenly became almost coy and hesitant, turning into a supplicant from the sure-of-herself boss she was a moment before.

"Please hold my hand," she said as she extended her right hand toward me. I looked at her with surprise. "I don't know if this is the best place," I started to say, but she interrupted me. "I just want to feel your energy," she said. "It gave me such a high last time. I have been thinking of it ever since. You have an extraordinary gift. Please, don't keep it all to yourself."

I smiled and took her hand between both of mine. The expression on her face immediately changed—she closed her eyes and visibly relaxed. A deep breath escaped her.

"That feels good," she sighed. She took another deep breath. I felt a surge of energy pass through me—I could feel it rising from the bottom of my spine, up my back and through the shoulders, down my arms and out through my hands into hers. I knew she had felt it too. It left me feeling weak, and I could sense my knees buckle under me. We stood there for a moment longer, then just as quickly as she had relaxed, Mrs. Grey snapped back into her usual get-up-and-go persona. She withdrew her hand.

"I need to sit down," I said. I could feel the blood draining from my face.

"Have a seat." Mrs. Grey indicated a chair that stood against the wall. I sat down.

"Are you all right?" she asked.

"I'm all right. I just need a moment to recover."

"Thank you for doing that. I feel so energized now."

I closed my eyes. I could still feel her energy coursing through me.

"Who is Robert?" I asked. I instinctively regretted asking the question but it just seemed to pop out of me. The name came into my head and just as soon as I received it, I said it.

"That's my son," Mrs. Grey said, looking concerned. "What are you seeing?" she asked.

"I don't know… It's not clear. But it has something to do with your health issues. Are you worried about him?" I opened my eyes and looked up at her.

"I am worried," she said. "He is married to a very selfish woman. She won't let him see me, even though they only live a short drive away in Connecticut. She seems to suck the energy right out of him."

"There are human vampires," I said. "Some people thrive on other people's energies. They don't give anything in return. You will know them because you will feel drained of energy after you have spent time with them."

"Oh, I know a few of those," Mrs. Grey confirmed.

"It's important to avoid such people," I said. I felt better and I stood up. "They can make you sick."

"Yes, but what if you are married to a vampire?" she asked. I shrugged my shoulders, as if getting rid of the contradiction. "I guess it's a choice," I said. "It's either them or you."

"Thank you for sharing your energy," Mrs. Grey said. "I hope you will be happy here at The Healthy Gourmet.

"I am sure I will," I assured her.

That afternoon Richard phoned to find out how my first day at work had gone.

"Really well," I said. "I think the job will work out."

He invited me out for dinner, but I wasn't sure whether this relationship wasn't going too fast. Besides, I had agreed to go to the movies with Bobbie.

"I'm busy," I said. "I'm going out with a friend."

"Then how about later tonight?"

"No, I'll be too tired."

But that evening, as Bobbie and I walked back to the apartment building, Richard was waiting at the front door of the building. I introduced him to Bobbie.

"Come on, let's go for a drink," he said. Bobbie seemed to be inclined to go.

"I'm tired," I said. "I must be at work at 8:30 tomorrow morning. You go. Enjoy."

Richard and Bobbie looked at each other, then at me. "It won't be the same without you," Bobbie said feebly, but I could tell the decision had been made.

"Really, it's fine," I assured them both. "I need an early night." We said goodnight and I let myself into the building as they walked away.

New York can be a lonely place but I intended to not submit to its loneliness. I knew that among the millions of New Yorkers who lived in the city or arrived in Manhattan every day from the remaining four boroughs or from Long Island, New Jersey or Connecticut there were those who wanted to understand about energies and the unseen worlds and who would share my passion for healing and helping others.

Where best to see those thousands of people arriving and departing every day, but at Grand Central Terminal? Over half a million people pass through the station each day, mostly on their way to somewhere else. Some take their time to look around.

I believe Grand Central Terminal is one of the most magnificent buildings in New York. It certainly is the most frequented building, and yet there are still aspects to it that are relatively unknown. It is a veritable cauldron of mixed energies, as all those people come and go through the terminal every day bringing their energy connections with them. If one could see the energies that are manufactured, processed and exchanged

In·sight: MOMENTS OF BEING

there each day, one would see swirling, multi-colored clouds hovering around and over people as they say their hellos and goodbyes, as they rush through the concourse in anticipation of the journey ahead of them or wait for a friend or a date under the large opal-faced clock that adorns the information booth in the middle of the expansive space.

I took to often walking though the station, taking a short cut from 42nd Street to Lexington Avenue. Sometimes, if I was early, or on my way home, I would stop and look into the shop windows. Other times I would just stand on the east balcony, on the steps leading up to the Apple store and watch the crowds as they hurried, mingled and passed across the expanse below.

I met Henry on that balcony. I was standing there one evening, taking a short break on my way home when this tall man in a long black coat and red scarf approached me.

"Where is the subway?" he asked in a foreign accent. I pointed to the passageway on the opposite side of the concourse. "It's over there," I said. "Just follow the signs." He seemed to hesitate. "Where are you from?" I asked.

"Is it that obvious that I am a foreigner?" he asked with a smile. "I have been living here for two years."

"I detect an accent, but I am not sure where you are from."

"I am a citizen of the world," he said. This was a surprising answer; I certainly did not expect it. "But as far as my heritage and place of birth are concerned, I am German," he said. "In German my name is Heinrich Adler. But you can call me Henry or Harry." We stood there on the balcony for a moment in silence, as if neither of us wanted to interrupt the other's thoughts. Then finally Henry said, "I don't know where the subway is but I do know a lot about Grand Central Terminal."

"Like what?" I asked.

"Look at the ceiling," he said. "Do you see the constellations against the blue background?"

"Yes," I said, not sure what he was getting at.

"Well, they are depicted..." he seemed to have trouble pronouncing the word *depicted*, "... shown backwards."

"What do you mean?" I asked.

"That's not the right sequence of constellations, if seen from the planet. However, if you were looking at the stars from outside the planet, from outside the galaxy, that's how you might see them. It's God's view of the heavens."

"How did that happen?" I asked, intrigued.

"Nobody knows," said Henry. "Maybe the artist was working from some Medieval manuscript, or perhaps he simply imagined he was looking at the heavens from the other side. Do you sometimes wonder what lies on the other side?" Henry looked me straight in the eyes and seemed to become very serious.

"Oh yes, daily," I joked. Then I added, "No, seriously, I have never in my life thought that we could reach outside the galaxy with our imagination. When I think about it, all I see is black space."

"Oh no, there is no such thing as empty space. The mind can travel wherever we decide to send it. We can go to the other side of the world in an instant. We can venture to the stars or to other planets. We can time travel as well—visit the future or check out the past. Wouldn't you want to be able to do that?"

"Of course I would. Who wouldn't?"

"Well, you can."

At that moment an image entered my head and I could see a young boy running through a forest landscape. I could see he was holding something in his hands, perhaps a ball or a toy. Then suddenly he tripped over a tree root and fell. He dropped the toy he was holding and screamed in pain. Another boy came running toward him and bent over him. Then suddenly the image disappeared. I noticed Henry was looking intently at me.

"What just happened?" he asked.

"Did you fall and break your leg when you were nine or ten- years-old?" I asked.

"Yes, I did," he said. It happened in a forest in Bavaria. After a moment he added, "I still walk with a slight limp."

"I am sorry," I said. "I saw it happen." Henry was obviously speechless, because he didn't say anything. He just stared at me. I broke the silence. "So what else do you know about this building?" I asked. "Apart from the fact that you can observe God's view of the universe?"

Henry sighed and pointed up to the ceiling. "I know that that black patch up there was left as a reminder after the ceiling was cleaned and repainted. It shows what it looked like before the renovations. Everyone thought the black coating on the ceiling was city grime and pollution but it turned out it was caused by cigarette smoke. Of course now you are not allowed to smoke in here or on the trains."

"How interesting," I said.

"I also know that the hole in the ceiling"—here he pointed to an indentation visible above the concourse—"was made during the Cuban missile crisis when a missile was brought in here and displayed for all to see. It was so high, they had to make a hole in the ceiling to fit it in its entirety." He paused for a moment and then continued. "Did you know there is a whisper gallery here in the station?"

"No, I did not."

"Let me show you." We climbed down from the balcony, continued under the east passage and took the escalator outside the Transit Museum downstairs. We walked through the food court to the passageway outside the Oyster Bar. Here Henry instructed me to stand on one side of the passage facing the wall, while he faced the other wall opposite and started whispering to the wall. I could hear every word, as if he were standing right next to me.

"Let's go in for a drink to the Oyster Bar and I'll tell you an interesting story."

"Yes, okay," I found myself responding to the wall. "But I only have half an hour." I turned around and there was Henry, standing before me with a great big grin on his face. I was surprised at myself for agreeing to go to a

Grand Central Terminal

bar with a stranger, but I felt I knew him from somewhere, only I could not remember from where.

We walked into the Oyster Bar which was not yet crowded and sat at the bar. We ordered cocktails and a dozen oysters.

"The Oyster Bar has been here since 1913, the same year the Grand Central Terminal first opened," Henry explained. "But it really became what it is today when the Transit Authority signed a lease with Jerome Brody who brought it back to splendor and introduced all these wonderful seafood dishes as well as over twenty varieties of oysters."

"Is that the story you were going to tell me?" I asked. "Not that I'm not interested in the history of restaurants and the Grand Central Terminal…"

"No, no," Henry laughed. "I wanted to tell you about Martin Luther."

"You mean the man who started the Reformation movement in Europe?" I asked.

"Yes, but did you know we owe the Christmas tree and Christmas tree decorations to his experience?"

"No, I did not. Tell me," I said.

"He was walking through the Black Forest in south-western Germany when suddenly he saw a tree that was illuminated by hundreds of colored balls. These were balls of energy and lines of force that looked like tinsel. On top of the tree there was a bright light. What he probably saw was some energy phenomenon that humans normally refer to as fairies or nature spirits. I have seen such a thing and it is magnificent to behold.

"So Luther chopped down a spruce tree and tried to recreate what he saw indoors. People in the village must have seen it and liked it, because by the 19th century the custom began to spread around the world."

"Where did you see this? What color were the lights?"

I saw it in Germany, walking through the forest one summer day. The lights were all colors of the rainbow and it rendered me speechless."

"That must have been wonderful. Do you still see energy around people or trees?" I asked.

"Sometimes, but not very often." He was about to say something more but suddenly there was someone standing behind us. It was Richard.

"What are you doing here?" he asked.

I turned around. "I could ask you the same thing," I said. I then introduced the two men to each other. "Henry, this is Richard. Richard, this is Henry." Richard sat down on a bar stool next to me.

"Can I buy you both a drink?" he asked.

"No, thank you, I need to go," I said.

Henry must have sensed the awkwardness of the situation. "I need to go, too," he said. "Barman," he called out to the young man behind the counter. "Can I have my bill, please?"

"Certainly," the barman responded.

"Don't rush off on my behalf," Richard said. Henry and I stood up. While Henry was paying the bill, Richard hissed at me, through his clenched teeth, "I really thought you were better than that." Henry must have heard him because he gathered up his change and swung round to face Richard.

"What did you just say?" he demanded.

"Nothing that concerns you," Richard replied.

"Apologize to Barbara immediately!"

"And what if I don't?"

"We can settle this matter outside, if you like."

"That won't be necessary," I chimed in. "Come on, Henry. Let's get going." I pulled him away by the sleeve. He resisted but in the end he relented. Richard was smiling, as if he had been victorious.

As we walked out of the restaurant, Henry said, "You should have let me deal with that guy. Who is he anyway?"

"Just a man I know. He calls himself a magician." Henry laughed. "Well, he didn't exactly behave like one, did he?"

"I wouldn't know. I've never met a magician before."

"I would think a magician should be able to control his emotions and behave more like a gentleman than a thug."

"I guess you are quite right," I said, as we walked back onto the concourse at Grand Central Terminal.

Chapter Eighteen

Wonder

In my dream that night something was wrong with the water system and I was sent to the pump to fetch a couple of pails of water, so that there could be enough to make the soup and wash the dishes. As I was carrying the full pails back, I noticed how heavy the water was and how the handles seemed to dig into my hands. I had to stop two or three times on the way and rub my hands together, attempting to smooth out the newly formed creases.

How much water do we use a day, I wondered. Of course, it depends where a person lives—whether there is an abundance of water or not, whether it is a hot and dry land, or wet and humid. From the moment we wake up, we drink it, wash with it, cook with it, clean with it, many, many times a day. I never think about carrying water from a well or a pump or a spring because it is always there, at my beck and call, at the ready in my kitchen or from the bathroom taps. However, it never used to be like that for our ancestors and they must have valued the life-giving substance more. Rarity produces value in the world and there has always been little appreciation for what exists in abundance, although the most precious substances on Earth are there in seemingly unlimited quantities.

I stood there for a minute and dipped the fingers of my right hand into the transparent liquid. It was cool and refreshing, having been recently

In·sight: MOMENTS OF BEING

pumped up from the earth; it felt cooling against my hot and tired hand.

It was strange to think that I too was mostly made of water and that therefore there was a natural affinity and bond between water and my human body. In that moment I understood why the native peoples of this continent would refer to water saying, "The river is my sister" or "The lake is my brother." I suddenly felt connected, supported and cared for with a sense of belonging. I realized I was an endemic part of this great universal appearance on and within planet Earth. It occurred to me that perhaps being human means to be a universal experiment and that we are on trial to see if we can establish the human specie as it was meant to be—living in harmony with our environment, with the Earth itself and with each other. I picked up my two buckets again and although they were still heavy, my load had definitely lightened, or so it seemed.

As I walked toward the kitchen door, I felt a great peace and settlement, as if I no longer had to become anything other than what I already was; I no longer had to prove myself or want more than I already had—I felt I was home because this beautiful and generous ball called Earth was my home and continued to provide me with everything I could ever want or need. In response I felt a new indebtedness, a sense of responsibility and compulsion to pay back, to be grateful and to process thoughts and feelings that would become food for her, just as she has always been willing to supply many levels of food for me. Water was one such example of a food and I became very conscious of the fact that there were many more. In fact, every breath, every sight, every sound, every meal and drink—everything I took into myself, providing it was not poisonous and was fit for human consumption, was a food that energized me and allowed me to live.

What could the Earth possibly want in return? Why did she support millions of us if all we did was take and transform her landscapes into pollution and devastation? What does she want? For the first time in my life I felt the planet to be a live, pulsating, developing being with her own wishes, desires, longings and aims. I felt it was up to me to find out what these were and to strike up a reciprocal relationship whereby I would continue to be fed, clothed and nurtured, but she would also receive something in return.

I stopped in my tracks and once again put down my heavy load. I suddenly realized that the planet needs to be fed as well and that we were here with her permission to provide a higher food, which only we could supply. It occurred to me that only humans, of all creatures on Earth, were potentially conscious enough to fetch from the universe a higher food, both for ourselves and for the planet we live on. I marveled at the fact that she provides the exact conditions for our sustainability. Doesn't she mix the ingredients to be found in the water, the air and the vegetation to give us exactly what we need to survive? Change the recipe even slightly and we would all be dead in an instant. And doesn't she always somehow compensate for our mismanagement of resources to give us yet another chance of survival?

Suddenly the revelation came to express itself in three words—she needs us! She needs human beings!

The fact that she spins ensures that her entire surface is warmed and nurtured by the life giving sun. This is her dedication and her constancy, for don't we rely on this regularity and even set our time measuring devices, called watches and clocks, according to this rotating repetitional movement? Perhaps my repayment to this life-giving force should also be constant and reliable and repetitional. Perhaps I could fashion myself according to her laws and precepts and contemplate often the wonder of this divine engineering. For as I stood there I felt I was an important ingredient in a greater plan and that in my own small way I was being influential in this universal pattern of growth, movement and development. It made my life feel worthwhile and even necessary, though not in a personal way that is subject to ambition and vanity. I felt, for the first time in my life, that I had a part to play in this universal plan and I was grateful to be alive.

As I walked into the kitchen, I noticed that everyone looked at me as if they had never seen me before and for the first time I became aware of two rivulets of tears making their way down my cheeks. They were tears of joy,

In·sight: MOMENTS OF BEING

relief and happiness, and I felt a new sense of hope and beginning.

I placed the buckets of water on the counter and Mary, the cook, poured one of them into a large bowl which she was using to wash dishes. As she did so, she looked at me intently with curiosity, but said nothing. She just smiled with recognition and proceeded to continue with her tasking of washing the dishes. I wiped away my tears with my sleeve and began cutting the lettuce for a salad. I noticed how green and fresh it looked and how bright and orange the carrots looked and how red and fresh the tomatoes looked. It was as if everything had taken on an iridescent quality, emanating a light from within. Everything I looked at was alive and in service to life; and I felt that I, too, was part of this great dedication.

In the evening I knocked on the Master's door, excited to tell him about my discovery. To my surprise he seemed to already know about what had happened that afternoon, and he was the one who started the conversation, "I hear you discovered awe today," he said.

I must have looked blank, for he did not wait for an answer, but continued, "Awe is a very necessary ingredient for you to have in your development. In fact, you cannot proceed beyond a certain point without it. It will give you the conductivity you need to connect to higher thoughts and feelings. It will reveal to you a sense of belonging and a great value for life in all its aspects, so that you may begin to pay back for your existence."

I could recognize the importance of awe and so I nodded my agreement. "Yes, this is exactly how I felt. I could begin to see that I have a part to play in the greater universal plan."

"Yes, you have glimpsed the truth. But it will take you a lifetime to adopt it and make it become a way of life. There are many temptations in the world that lure us away from these contemplations and you will need to struggle to make time and room for them. Perhaps that is why there are so many human beings on the planet at this time, so that at least some can bring the gift of consciousness to this otherwise deserted place. For every thought, every deed, every feeling carries with it an energetic charge that either feeds the planet, and all those who are in receipt of it, or detracts from it."

He paused for a moment and then added, "We are looking for the human beings of tomorrow. They are already here today and they live by awe and wonder and value—they are not here to destroy but to find a way to pay back for their existence. This is the only way to ensure continuance after the death of the physical body. I see you are on the right track. Remember today's lesson well, for it will provide you with the foundation from which to proceed into your next level of development. For how can you collect the essences of care or service or honesty or patience, if you do not value your own existence? Charity begins at home, they say, but so does hope and trust and belief and every other essence quality you can name. How can you value yourself if you do not value the planet you live on or the universe you have been born into? Find a way to remind yourself often of this discovery and you will be able to proceed into greater tasks that will reveal more to you, for this is just the beginning."

The Master held out his hand. "There are many levels of energy," he said. "As I hold out my hand, I could be touching a thought form that was left here from yesterday or I might be intercepting the energy of an angel or a nature spirit. They can both live in the same space, at different times or in different dimensions.

"Planetary energy exists at seven levels," he explained. "The lowest level contains the energies of criminal behavior, warfare, murders and abuse. The next level is the level of ongoing life, habitual behavior, maintenance and the struggle for survival. Level five is to do with education and self development. But what you encountered today was the experience of elevating to level four where nature spirits and healing energies live. Level three is the angelic realm and two and one is where divinity emanates from. You have been blessed today. You now know that there are many levels of experience to be had on planet Earth. It all depends on who you are, your education and whether you are open to awe and wonder."

With that he stopped and I realized that the interview was over. Elated from the day's process, I left the study and returned to my room.

From that day on something changed in my outlook on life and its purpose. I felt that the answers I was looking for were inside me and I knew that my constant search for the next understanding or the next truth would no longer be directed at everything and everyone I met, for it was there to be uncovered and discovered within me.

I felt I now had the tools with which to proceed—I needed only to retrace my thoughts into that cavern of wonder to find therein many jewels—value for life wherever it may be found, and above all, a sense of a purpose and a greater plan.

All this was still not fully formulated in me but it did bring with it a settlement and an ease, when realizing that no life is in vain because all are here for a reason and it is for each person to discover their unique calling and purpose.

I also noticed that my conversations with the Master were taking on a different tone and resonance—I felt less of a student and more a companion on this development journey called life. I also started writing and meditating, which were tools and methods to stay connected to the unfolding picture of divine will. I began to see how the human has the choice to pursue their humanity and divinity or not and that this choice is for each person to make.

I wanted to not be parted from what I felt that day when I carried the two buckets of water from the pump to the kitchen, for at that moment my senses were heightened as never before and I saw the beauty of the world in a new light, with new colors and hues, vibrancies and radiations that I had never noticed before. The incandescent, iridescent, glimmering and shimmering sights I had witnessed felt now more real than the mundane pictures I had been accustomed to before.

But for now this was only a memory and I felt I needed to find the tools to get back to that state in which both my senses and my thinking had been enhanced as never before.

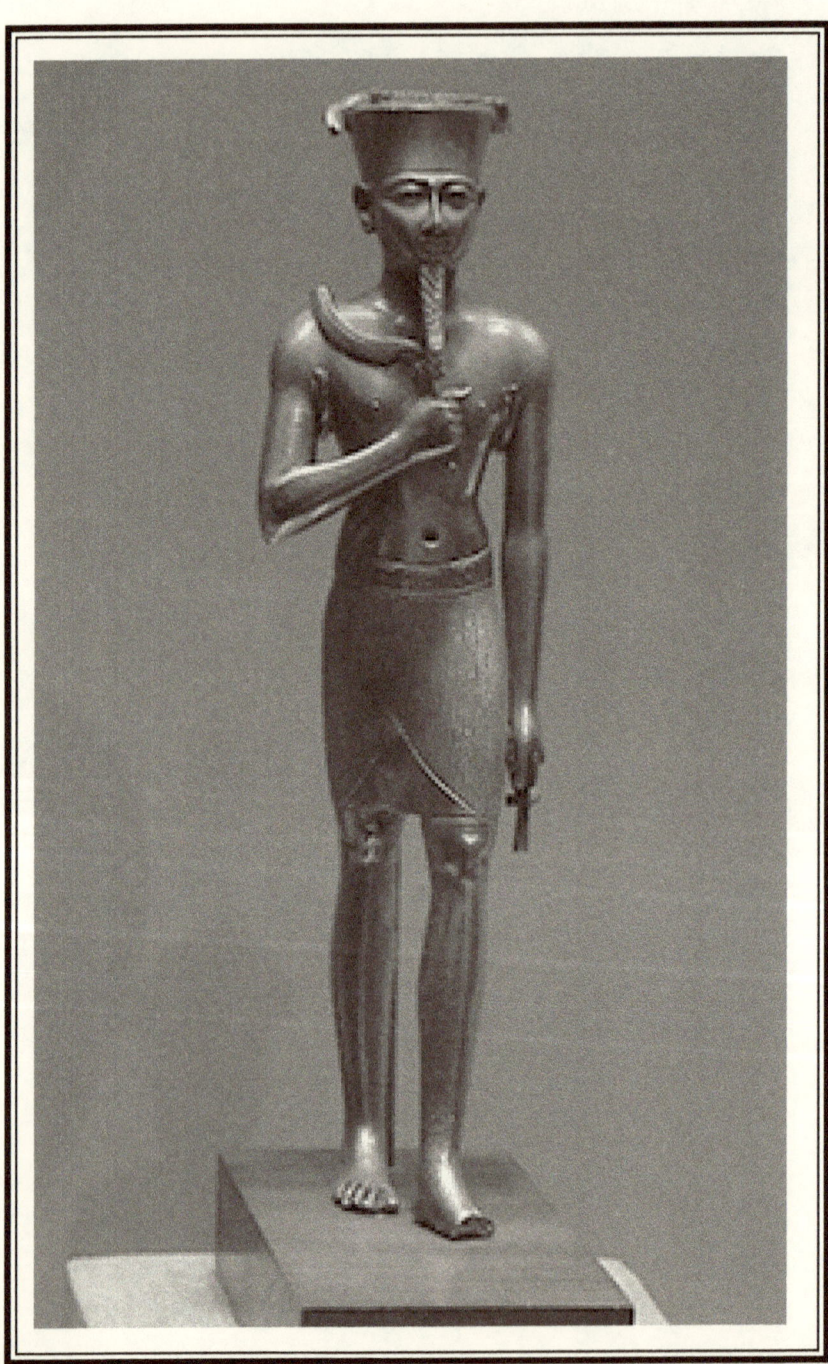

Chapter Nineteen

The MET

A few days later Mrs. Grey came into the office and asked me to meet her for lunch. We met at a little Thai restaurant on 44th Street. I sensed she had something urgent to tell me.

As soon as we sat down, she began. "I went to see my doctor yesterday," she said. "They took an X-ray and couldn't find the cancer. The doctor asked the radiologist to come in as well and they both could not believe that there is nothing there. They still want me to take radiation treatment as a precaution, but I say, to hell with them, I am not going to do it. I know I am cured and I know why. You did it. You are the healer."

I swallowed hard. I did not expect this. "Are you sure?" I asked.

"Of course I am," she answered. Then she added, "The world needs to know about you and your ability to heal."

"Oh, I don't know about that. I am no healer. I would rather call myself an energy worker."

"But think of all the good you can do in the world. Cancer is a major killer, you know. Your energy could cure thousands."

"Slow down, Marjorie." It was the first time I called her by her first name. "I know I can channel energies that heal. But I am only one person and there is only so much one person can do. I think I am meant to teach others how to heal themselves, rather than going around hospitals healing everyone."

Mrs. Grey took a deep breath. "Maybe you're right," she said. "I am sure you know best. I got carried away there for a minute."

"I think it is significant that we are having this conversation," I said. "Do you want to be a healer? Do you want to learn about energies? Maybe you could help me reach a larger number of people. I want people to know they can heal themselves."

We were interrupted by the waiter who came up to our table to take our orders. We quickly scanned the menu and made our decisions. As soon as the waiter left, Mrs. Grey leaned forward and said, "Yes, I think the fact that I beat this cancer means that I can help others do the same."

"Good. In that case we need to consider how we are going to go about getting the information into the world."

"Well, I have worked in public relations for years. I would say you need a website so people can find you on the Internet and you need a brochure."

"Okay, that sounds like a good beginning. What should the brochure say?"

Mrs. Grey pulled out a notebook and a pen and suddenly she was all business. "How about we say, 'Heal Yourself,'" she suggested.

"That sounds good, but I've heard it a thousand times already. We should come up with something more original. It's more than just about healing, isn't it? It's about understanding energies and the laws that govern them. It's also about showing people how they can see, feel, touch and experience energies. Energy is as real as the material world."

"I'm beginning to get a sense of that," Mrs. Grey said.

By the end of the meal we had a first draft of a brochure and we had put together some basic ideas for a website. I felt Mrs. Grey was the right person to get things started and that we could work well together.

I never intended to be a teacher. But perhaps one's real calling is the one that happens without planning, simply because one can do nothing else.

The attempt to reach people escalated when I met Mandy. Mandy was a waitress at my local diner. I became accustomed to going there to sit with a cup of coffee and read my e-mails because they had free wifi which was sadly lacking at the apartment. One day, as I approached the cashier's station situated at the entrance to the diner to pay my bill, I overheard Mandy who was standing behind the cashier, talking on her cell phone.

"You are always saying that," she said, and she was obviously upset. Then she became quiet and put her phone in her pocket. I paid my bill and watched her out of the corner of my eye as she walked toward the back of the restaurant. As I was leaving, she suddenly appeared on the street and stood close to me, lighting a cigarette. I couldn't help remembering a lesson my grandmother had taught me about arguing successfully.

"I couldn't help hearing you speak over the phone," I said. The girl looked up at me in surprise. She didn't say anything, obviously waiting for me to continue.

"There are two words you should never say during an argument," I continued.

"Oh, and what are they?" she asked.

"Never and always," I replied. "Never say never and never say always."

"And why is that?" the girl asked again.

"They are too final. It is also simply not true. No one says or does something always. Often might be a better word. And besides, in an argument you should always discuss one incident or one issue at a time and not bring into it past history and other events."

"So how do you know all this? Are you a psychologist?" she asked. Memories of my grandmother were coming back to me. What came out of my mouth, though, surprised me; I have no idea why I said it.

"I am a teacher."

"Then tell me, teacher, how can I deal with someone who keeps telling me I am stupid and immature?"

"Well, are you?" I asked.

"I guess sometimes I am," she admitted.

"Then perhaps you can admit that you sometimes are and take steps to grow up and become more responsible. Perhaps you can ask your boyfriend..." The girl looked at me in surprise.

"Oh yes, I know you were talking to your boyfriend. I know a lot of things about people. Sometimes I wish I didn't. So perhaps you can ask your boyfriend to help you and give you advice, rather than becoming frustrated with you and calling you names. But if you do, you will also need to follow through and follow his advice, once you agree to do so."

Her eyes grew large in disbelief.

"How do you know he is my boyfriend?" she asked.

"Well, that was obvious from the way you were talking to him on the phone."

"It was that obvious?" It was more a statement than a question. There was a moment of silence during which I pondered whether indeed it was that obvious or whether some instinct had kicked in and somehow I just knew the girl had been talking to her boyfriend on the phone.

"I have to go now," she said as she crushed her cigarette butt under foot. "But I would love to learn more. Can you teach me?" I was not prepared for this. I hesitated.

"Please," the girl pleaded. "Here is my number." She pulled out a notepad from her waitress's pouch she was wearing and wrote her phone number down for me. "My name is Mandy. Call me." She handed me an order slip with the restaurant logo and her number on it, and before I could say anything, she had turned around and walked back into the restaurant through the kitchen door.

It took a week before I saw Mandy again. Initially I had no intention of phoning Mandy. In fact, I forgot all about her as I went about my business. But a few days later when I went back to the diner for a light lunch, Mandy was my waitress. As soon as she came to my table, instead of asking for my order, she enquired, "How do you know so much about people?"

"I just do," I replied. "I always knew what people's intentions were and what their weaknesses were. Just look around," I said, glancing at the tables and scrutinizing the busy lunch crowd. "That man by the window with the large nose and red cheeks has a drink problem," I said. "That might be pretty obvious, but what is not obvious is that his wife has threatened to leave him and he is suffering from acute depression." Mandy followed my glance and I continued. "The couple in the corner are not girlfriend and boyfriend or man and wife. They are business partners and they are working out their monthly projections. He fancies her but she is married and he knows he hasn't got a chance. The older woman sitting on her own is a widow. She is terribly lonely but too shy to ask any of her late husband's friends to meet her for dinner or a movie. I could go on but I don't like to intrude into other people's affairs." I looked at Mandy. She smiled.

"It must be wonderful to be able to do that," she said with a sigh.

"Quite the opposite," I retorted. "I don't want to know about people's private affairs. But it's like a curse; I just do."

"I would love to be able to do that," said Mandy as she took the order pad out of her apron pocket. "What can I get you today?" she asked, assuming her professional stance and tone.

"Just a salad," I said. "The Greek salad," I added.

When Mandy brought the bill to the table, she asked to meet me. "Just for a few hours," she said. "I really need to know more."

I recognized the girl's genuine need and interest, so without thinking about it for very long, I agreed.

"Come to my place on Monday," I said and I wrote down the address on a napkin. I sat there for a moment, uncertain what had just taken place. Was this a folly or a beginning of a new life and a new career? Would I be able to teach this girl and if so, what was the curriculum supposed to be? But something in me was settled and deep down I knew that this was exactly the right next step for me and that all would be well.

At first I was unsure whether I should meet Mandy or cancel our appointment, but a few nights after I met her for the second time I had a dream which sealed my fate. I dreamed I was in a large auditorium addressing several hundred people. It was one of those dreams that felt very real and when I woke up I did wonder whether it was just a dream or whether in fact I had visited the future.

When the appointed time came, there was a knock on the door. She was punctual—that was a good sign. I was surprised that I had not heard the buzzer prior to her arrival upstairs and when I opened the door, I was even more surprised—she was standing there together with a young man at her side.

"Someone opened the downstairs door with a key," she explained, no doubt noticing my surprise, "so we came right up." After a moment's silence, she proceeded with the introductions. "This is my boyfriend Adam," she said. "He is the one I was speaking to the other day on the phone," she added, in an effort to jog my memory.

"Oh yes, I remember," I said. "Do please come in."

They both stepped into the apartment.

"Let me take your coats," I said as I opened the hall closet door.

When we emerged into the living room I offered them a cup of tea. The water had already been boiled so it did not take me long to bring out a pot of green tea and a few cookies. As I was distributing the mugs with tea, Mandy confessed, "I invited a few of my friends," she said. "I thought it would be easier for you to teach a small group, rather than just concentrating on Adam and me."

"That was thoughtful of you," I replied. "But it would have been better to check with me first."

"I was afraid you might say no," Mandy replied. She did not appear to be phased at all.

"Now we will never know, will we?" I replied with a smile. I don't know whether she understood that I was implying that she had not given me the freedom to choose whether I wanted a larger audience or not. My hint was perhaps too subtle for her.

"They are really nice people," Adam ventured into the conversation. I sensed he wanted to diffuse the situation, and that he understood how I felt and what I had meant.

Over the next half hour six more people arrived—all invited by Mandy. First came her sister, then two waitresses from the diner where Mandy worked, then an older couple who were friends of her parents and finally one of Adam's friends. I ran out of mugs, chairs and cookies but no one seemed to mind. They sat on the floor and the sofa, the armchair and the four dining room chairs—every seat was occupied.

Nine is a good number, I thought to myself, trying to remain positive about the fact that they were all expecting me to deliver a good show. I decided not to disappoint them and to demonstrate my clairvoyance to get their attention.

"Okay, let's start," I said, looking around the room at the eager looks of expectation. "What an interesting gathering of people. The one aspect you all seem to have in common is curiosity and a hunger for knowledge. It is to your credit that you have kept that quality alive and that you want to understand about the worlds of energy and unseen powers and forces, which are just as real as the material worlds, though invisible to the eyes.

"Let me demonstrate," I continued. "Hold out your hands." They all did so, even though they did not know what I intended to do. I held out my left arm, with the fingers pointing downwards and went around the room transmitting energy from my hand into theirs. What then happened surprised even me. Mandy's sister, who was sitting on the floor, stood up to make it easier for me to reach her outstretched hand. As I pointed my fingers into her palm, she gave out an exclamation of surprise and took a step backwards.

"Wow, that was so strong," she said. "Amazing," she added as she sat back down on the floor. "It really threw me backward. It was like a live current."

"Yes, exactly," I confirmed as I completed the circuit around the room.

"Did you feel that?" I addressed the whole group. They all nodded affirmatively in response.

In·sight: MOMENTS OF BEING

"What did it feel like?" I asked again.

"Pins and needles," Adam's friend replied.

"It was warm," Mandy added.

"It was like a breeze," the older woman offered.

"What was it?" asked Mandy's sister.

"It's energy," I responded, as I sat back down in a chair. "Every person on Earth who is alive processes energy. It comes from the Earth and it is a natural part of the human heritage. Depending on who you are, what you have done in your life, what you think about and what are your priorities, the energy increases or diminishes. That is why some people find they have healing abilities while others suffer from low energy and exhaustion."

To demonstrate my point, I asked for a volunteer. Alice, one of the waitresses from the diner put her hand up. I asked her to come out to the middle of the room. I asked her to hold her right arm out and to resist me when I tried to push it down. She was strong but I managed to push her arm down to her side. I then asked her to think about something good that had happened in her life, like passing an exam or completing a project and again I tested her strength. This time I was unable to push her hand hardly at all. I finally asked her to think of something that did not go so well for her and her arm dropped almost the moment I touched it. In response, there were gasps of awe from the small gathering.

I then asked if anyone felt any pain. Rosa, Mandy's sister put her hand up. "My foot hurts," she said. I fell off a stool yesterday and it is very bruised. I don't think I broke anything but I can hardly walk. I asked her to come out and sit on a chair. I then asked her to place her foot on another chair which was offered by Adam's friend who then sat down in front on the floor. I held my hand over Alice's foot and I could clearly feel heat emanating from her heel. I endeavored to pull the heat away, out of her aura. It took several swipes but I could feel the cooling effect of my actions. Alice felt it too. "That feels better," she said with a sigh.

When she stood up, she gently placed her foot on the floor. She then took a couple of steps and looked at me in disbelief.

The MET

"That's amazing," she said. "It hardly hurts at all."

"That is the healing power," I said. Every one of you can be a healer. You simply need to learn how to do it and practice."

"I saw green energy coming out of your hand when you did that," Adam's friend said.

I smiled, because I could see it too. "That is the healing force," I confirmed.

It is strange how sometimes the course of one's life gets decided in a moment, although mostly one can trace the origins of that single moment throughout one's history, like a motif snaking its way through years of longing. So it was with me when at the end of our modest gathering Rosa, Mandy's sister, asked, "So when is the next meeting?"

We were all standing by the door and a hush fell over the gathering as an air of expectancy descended and all eyes turned toward me. Instinctively I knew this was an important moment and that the decision as to whether to continue was entirely mine to make.

"Let's meet again next Tuesday at 8 P.M," I found myself saying and to this day I am not sure which part of my brain, mind or soul had intervened and supplied that answer. It tripped off my tongue so easily. The moment it was said, I realized that I had not given a thought to the consequences of my utterance. How would I accommodate a group in my small New York apartment? What could I teach them? Where were the study materials coming from? Who would write the curriculum?

At the time, none of this seemed to matter. The moment I had finished the sentence, a palpable feeling of relief rose from within the midst of the small group hovering at the threshold of the apartment. Suddenly there were hugs, goodbyes and expectations to reunite in a few days' time.

Once everyone had left, I sat down and started to write a list of all the things I would need before the following Tuesday. Such items as mugs, tea and cookies were on the list, but above all, I needed direction and a sense of order. People who study—people who have gone to school or are still at school—expect to follow a program, to learn about A before B, to count up to five before moving on to double digits, to discover their local town or province before learning about the world. Babies learn to walk before they can run and athletes need to train before they can compete in the Olympics. So how do you teach someone about energy, healing and using one's intuition and sixth sense, also known as ESP, in a progressive, ordered manner?

There is something spontaneous and forever changing about the worlds of energy—every experience is unique and different. So it is impossible to corral one's knowledge into a workbook or form of study that could serve as a template for all. And yet, I also realized that there could be some basic exercises, ways and means to help a person harness their sensitivity so they could gain an insight into the unseen worlds of energy.

Every living person on Earth has a body, a brain, a mind, a soul and a spirit. If I could find ways to train these living organs and one's five senses to feel, touch, see and respond to the worlds of energy, then perhaps I could indeed develop a program that could work for those who wanted to live in harmony with the planetary energies that sustain them on a daily basis.

At the weekend I went to the Metropolitan Museum of Art and visited the Egyptian section. There is a majesty and timelessness about Egyptian art that always makes me feel at peace with myself and the world. Once there, I felt like all was well and that I was doing exactly what I was supposed to be doing. I had gone there in search of cues, because much of Egyptian art was inspired by the worlds of energy. The shapes, colors and hieroglyphs are energetic symbols that offer clues as to the way the ancient Egyptians lived their lives and what were their priorities.

I was standing in front of one particular statue when I noticed that the eyes did not seem to be looking at any particular point in front of them, but had a long distance, almost detached look. I also noticed that the statue of the man had one foot forward, one hand closed and the other hand was holding what looked like a round bar. I had read somewhere that the

The MET

Egyptians used to hold metal magnets to boost their energy. The man was standing very erect and he looked as if he had been standing there for eons and eons of time. He was wearing a large pectoral around his neck. I took on a similar posture and adopted a long distance look. People were walking by, but I just stood there, looking long distance, letting my eyes gaze to the end of the gallery and then even further, through the wall, through the next gallery and on, out of the museum, through New York and out to the end of the Earth. Just as Richard Raven had explained to me, I realized, as I was standing there, that I had always been taught and instructed to focus—to look at the teacher or my notebook, a book, a blackboard or a computer screen. All my life I had been looking at flowers, trees, people, faces, rooms, clothes, interiors, movies, but never really letting my eyes un-focus and never taking on this, what seemed like an eternal, look. It reminded me of the look that Richard had shown me when I had met him at Cleopatra's Needle in Central Park, just a few steps away from where I now stood.

As I continued adopting this stance and as I relaxed into it some more, something very strange happened. Suddenly I began to see swirling masses of energy. I could see, as people walked by, that each person was emanating a whole mass of energy—through their hands, the top of their heads, out of their eyes, their face and even through their clothing all over their bodies. Soon I could see light around people and objects as well, until finally the noise grew quieter and I began to see color. As the hues became more visible and pronounced, the physical bodies began to disappear and a few moments later all I was seeing were clouds of energy entering my field of vision and then disappearing again.

The range and number of shades of colors was enormous—some people were surrounded by dark clouds, while others were emanating pastel shades and vibrant hues. I could almost see what each person was energetically attached to—whether they were healthy or in pain and whether they were in a good mood or perhaps worried about something. It was an extraordinary display and it probably only lasted for a few minutes, but it felt like an eternity to me.

"Wow," I thought, "if only I could teach this to other people, it would no doubt change their lives forever." To see clouds of energy like this and to realize that we emanate, manufacture, process and exchange energy all the time is to understand that the physical body is simply a processing plant for energy.

I slowly came out of the posture and looked around me. The gallery was still there, the people were milling around and reading inscriptions describing individual artifacts, but I was feeling as if the world had changed. At least my world had changed. I picked up my bag and started to walk toward the entrance to the next gallery, wondering about what had just happened, when I noticed a man standing in the corner looking intently in my direction. As I approached the exit, he started walking towards me. I stopped and turned to face him as it became obvious that he was going to speak to me.

"I hope you don't mind," he said as he approached me, "but I noticed you standing there next to that statue." He pointed at the statue I had been imitating in my posture. I waited for him to continue.

"There was something different about you. I could see a light around your head and light coming out of your eyes. I've never seen anything like that before. What was that?"

"I don't know," I replied. "I could see light around people, too, but I have no idea why. I was simply taking on the posture of that statue."

"I think you have special capabilities," the man said. "You must be a healer."

"Who are you?" I asked.

"I'm a sparrow," the man said. I thought I had misheard him.

"Did you say sparrow?" I asked. "Isn't that a bird?"

"Yes. It's a bird at the beginning of his esoteric studies. No fancy plumage, no melodious birdsong, just your basic bird learning humility and the skill of listening."

"So what are you doing here?"

"The ancient Egyptians had a very advanced civilization. They have left us numerous clues in their artwork, buildings and hieroglyphs. Take, for example, this statue." He pointed to a small statue of a man on a pedestal. "If you take on the posture that this man has adopted, you will feel a surge of energy. Try it." I did. He showed me how to roll my shoulders up, back and down, how to stand with one foot forward and roll up my fingers by my side, at the same time projecting forward energy through my thumbs. I immediately felt a wave of energy, causing tingling in my hands.

"That's amazing," I said. "I feel it. It feels like I've been connected to an electrical current."

"That's right," Sparrow said. It's planetary energy you are connecting to. If you look around this gallery, you will see these are not just Egyptian postures; they are human postures. And yet how different to our own.

"Let me show you something else," he said as he went through the entrance to the next gallery and I followed him. "These statues hold enormous power," he said as we stood in front of a statue of a man sitting with a hawk attached to the back of his head. "The hawk is the hunter and the forager. If it appears in a man's energy field, it means that he is someone whose brain is being enhanced by an energetic form—this man is a leader and an evolved being. He has wisdom and can command healing energies. These forms which you can see in Egyptian artwork above people's heads were not physical—they never found a hat or headdress like this in any of the tombs. These are energy forms and they are very real. A hawk is a high energetic being."

I felt it was no coincidence that I had met Sparrow, having already encountered the art of Finch, the knowledge of Heron and the wisdom of Raven or Merlin.

"Thank you for sharing your information," I said. "That was an amazing lesson."

"That is what we birds are meant to do," replied Sparrow. "The world needs this knowledge and people need to be educated in the ways and means of the energy worlds. His words stirred something deep within me and now I knew that I needed to continue in my journey toward becoming a teacher of the unseen worlds.

Chapter Twenty

Persistence

That night my astral adventure at the mystery school continued. I had been summoned to meet the Master in the garden. It was early morning and we stood on the large lawn which stretched from the back of the school building, down a gentle slope toward a stream beyond. He was leaning on an old-fashioned scythe when I approached him. I stood quietly for a moment, awaiting my instructions.

"Your tasking today is simple, though arduous," he said with a smile. "I want you to cut the grass with this scythe." I looked around me and estimated that the lawn must have covered around three acres. I remained silent, awaiting further information.

"Yes, it is an ancient tool," he agreed with my silent query. "But it is effective and the whirring of a motor will not disturb your contemplations. I will see you when you are finished," he added as he handed me the scythe. I took it from him and held it awkwardly for a moment, not knowing what to do next. I had seen paintings and movies depicting this ancient object, but I realized I would first need to learn how to master it.

"You will find the way of it," he said. "You will be given food and drink when it is time to rest. You will also be given a metal bar with which you will be able to sharpen the blade." Clearly he had thought of everything. Before his departure, he added, "Think what quality you are learning about this day and let me know when you are finished." With that he turned around and left me in the middle of the lawn, wondering where to start. The first thought that came to my mind was, "Clearly the quality I will be learning is hard work," but I brushed it aside, deciding to give the process a chance to impress itself upon me.

So, where shall I start? I thought as I took hold of the scythe and turned it around so that the blade faced the ground. The scythe wasn't that heavy, but it would clearly take some effort to swing it from side to side. I didn't want anyone to see me practicing, so I decided to start at the far end of the lawn, where the ground began to slope down toward the small stream that lazily wound its way across the property.

From there the lawn looked even larger and my task more impossible. I wondered whether I should start at all or whether to declare myself unfit even before I attempted to tackle the task of cutting the grass which had grown to be above ankle level. Then I looked again at the scythe and decided it would be of historical interest to attempt to use it; I would then know what it had been like to harvest the grain centuries ago when the first settlers arrived here, tilled the land and collected their crops.

And so I started. Awkward at first, I soon got into the rhythm of the tool and felt that there was a certain harmony building between myself and it. I had no intention of either completing the job or even making a serious attempt at it; I just wanted to give it a little bit of time so I could honestly say that I had tried, but that it had been an impossible task to fulfill. As I continued, I found that pictures formed up in my mind and I felt transported into some Medieval Bruegel-like landscape. It was a strange dream state within a dream and I felt very comfortable within it. I was no longer me... that is, I was no longer Barbara, training to become more knowledgeable about myself and the world; I was a farmer or a farmer's wife, concerned about the crops, the weather, the fictitious landowner and the future. I felt I had traveled back in time. Everything seemed to change around me and I almost expected the squire to come riding by on horseback, to check whether my work was being done properly. And so I continued, lost in my reverie, one step at a time—systematically, progressively moving on. Just one more row, one more patch... I hardly noticed the sun creeping up the firmament above and before I knew it, it was shining high in the sky.

I stopped for a moment—it was hot and the work had been persistent. Not being used to it, my muscles ached. I stretched and paused, noticing that I was thirsty as well. And then I saw a figure in the distance walking toward me. A girl was carrying a basket in one hand and a jug in the other. Clearly she was heading straight for the very spot on which I stood, now resting my weight on the scythe. I waited for a moment and then I realized—she was bringing me refreshments!

She was a young girl, younger than me; she had a spring in her step and a smile on her face as she approached; her hair was tied back in a pony tail which cantered from side to side with each step as she walked. I was right, for as she came nearer, she explained that she was bringing me lunch.

"I've got some sandwiches for you," she said, "and a jug of water. Take a break, you must be tired." She looked around, admiring the results of my work. I took the jug from her and she handed me a cup which she had retrieved from the basket which was now resting on the ground.

"Thank you," I said, following her gaze and realizing that indeed, a large part of the field had been cut; in fact it was more than half. I looked at my hands and for the first time I noticed that there were blisters under two of my fingers on each hand. The girl followed my gaze and also looked at my hands and then she said, looking up at my face, "I have a message for you from the Master. He asked me to tell you not to continue, if you don't want to. He says he is satisfied with what you have done so far."

The water tasted so good—there is nothing quite as pure and fresh and clean as the taste of water when you are thirsty. It certainly is the purest and most wholesome of all drinks. I felt it replenish my strength and add to my vitality. I decided I was not going to quit now.

"Thanks for the message," I said, "but I would like to do just a little bit more and see how far I can get today."

"Suit yourself," the girl said, shrugging her shoulders, but without irritation. "I'll leave you the jug, the cup and the sandwiches, as well as the scythe sharpener." She pulled the last two items out of the basket and placed them on the ground as she was speaking. "I'll take the basket back. See you later," she added cheerfully as she picked up the basket and started to retrace her steps, swinging the empty basket as she went.

I looked at the field. "I'll just do a little bit more before I eat," I thought and started to cut away at the grass again, holding the scythe slightly differently so as to avoid cutting open the blisters on my hands. I was really enjoying the whole weave of the ingredients of fresh air, manual labor, the smell of the cut grass, the light breeze and the warm caress of the sun which, having reached the height of noon, was now slowly declining toward the west. And now there was another ingredient to make it more enjoyable—I didn't have to complete the work assigned to me. I was doing it because I wanted to and nobody but myself was going to decide how long and how intensively I needed to continue.

The afternoon went very quickly and before I knew it, the sun was setting and I had finished. I surveyed the field with great satisfaction, hardly believing that I had done it, on my own, and that I had actually enjoyed it. Looking back at the fruits of my labor I was surprised I had accomplished it on my own, it seemed impossible to do. But doing it bit by bit made it possible. Because it was a challenge, a novelty and an exercise in self-discovery, the many little efforts added up and here I was, the tasking accomplished! What else, I wondered, could I do that I had thought to be impossible, if only I applied the same method of progressing one step at a time? It made me think about the times in childhood, when carrying a heavy load, I would walk home from lamp post to lamp post, thus cutting down my journey each time to a manageable size. When you can see the end of a tasking, it is so much easier to begin.

I smiled as I picked up the scythe, the cup and the metal sharpener, as well as the now empty jug and walked back to the garden shed which was next to the schoolhouse. Once relieved of the tools, I took the jug back to the kitchen where I knew it was normally stored. Then suddenly I felt very tired and my arms and legs started to ache and felt heavy. It was that tired satisfaction one feels having completed a job well done.

Next I took a shower and put on some fresh clothes; although the bed looked like a very tempting proposition, I knew it was almost time for dinner, so I figured I had just enough time to see the Master and tell him about my day's discovery. I knocked on the office door and there he was—sitting at a desk. As I entered he looked at me with expectation and a sense of inquiry.

"So what did you learn today?" he asked.

I sat down in the chair opposite him and proceeded to explain, "I learned that there are many ways to look at a tasking—one is to take it all on at once and run the risk of being intimidated by the enormity of effort required to complete it, and the other is to simply take on what one can, a little at a time, but in a persistent manner, and then so much more can be achieved than I had ever imagined."

That really was the learning of the day. But the Master had something more to say. "Yes, I see you have learned the virtue of persistence. There is incredible power in that one word. Think of the blade of grass struggling against a layer of concrete—a million small efforts in the same direction—push, push, push, and eventually the concrete will crack and the small blade of grass will be released to rejoin the air and the sunlight. If this small piece of vegetation can do so much over time, think what you can achieve! The blade of grass never gives up and neither should you, ever."

He paused for a moment and just as I was wondering whether I should get up and leave, he continued, "The lessons you are learning are everywhere—in nature, in human behavior, in the way Creation and the universe are ordered. But think, do you see them? And if you do, do you ascribe to them the importance I am attempting to demonstrate to you now? You see, the fact that I am here, and you report to me after every tasking is fulfilled, makes your thoughts and actions seem important. You think you have to contemplate what you are going to say before you walk through that door. However, I will not always be around and you have your own teachers inside, one of them being your intuition. Learn to listen to it and follow its instructions, as if you were listening to me and your lessons may continue for as long as you are alive on this planet."

Chapter Twenty-One

The Rubin Museum

"You did what?" asked Mrs. Grey next morning when I told her about the meeting and the healing I had demonstrated the previous evening. I could tell she was annoyed. We were sitting in her office while she was checking in with me how I was getting on with the work.

"And you didn't invite me?" she asked.

"I didn't think you would want to come," I said.

"Well, you thought wrong." She was obviously very disappointed.

"In your condition, I thought it was better for you not to be in a room with all these mixed energies swirling around."

"What condition?" she snapped. "There is nothing wrong with me. I am fine."

I looked at her, surprised. "Did you hear from the doctor?" I asked.

"I did," she said and she smiled faintly. "They can't find anything. My lungs are clear."

"That's wonderful," I said, sounding perhaps a little too enthusiastic. I was glad we had changed the subject and were talking about her instead.

"Yes, it is," she confirmed. "But I already knew that. I am now ready to become engaged in your healing venture."

"What I want to do is to teach people how to heal themselves. With practice everybody can be a healer."

"No, no, no," she protested. "That way you are not going to make any money. You have to be the healer so people are dependent on you and have to come back again and again so you can charge them every time they come. That's what most healers do."

"That's not true," I responded. "The healing energy is a gift from the universe and I would not feel comfortable growing rich from other people's misfortunes."

"Well, you're going to have to charge them something. After all, you are giving people your time and energy."

"That's true, but I see myself to be a teacher rather than a healer." I paused for a moment and added, "If we are to work together, we need to agree about what the mission is."

"Well, let's agree that the mission is to teach and heal. That way we cover all bases."

"All right," I agreed, with some hesitation. Very aware that we were sitting in her office and talking during our work hours, I added, "We need to talk about this some other time."

"How about tonight?" Mrs. Grey was quick to respond. "I want to show you a draft of a brochure I have been working on."

I could see she meant business. Although for a moment I had felt like walking out of the office and disengaging from working with her, I could now see I needed her help, if I was to reach a large number of people. I felt it was my duty to put the information out into the world, but I could also see that it was my duty to direct the energy of whatever this mission was turning out to be and to be responsible for its integrity.

That evening me met at the little Thai restaurant near the apartment. Mrs. Grey brought with her a design of a brochure, which included a description of my work as well as a design of a logo. The logo showed the figure of a human in schematic form, surrounded by a multi-colored aura that seemed to shimmer and glow with radiance and health. It looked nice and I had

The Rubin Museum

to admit she had done a great job. Clearly, she understood the market and knew how to appeal to a wide audience.

Becoming a commercial venture in today's world does require a certain degree of compromise. It is easy to be honest and saintly in a Himalayan cave, but if one wants to reach a large number of people, one does need to advertise and find a description that gives justice to the service one is offering and is appealing enough to cause a response.

"Brochures are all very well," Mrs. Gray said, "but in today's fast moving world you need video and you need to reach people on the Internet. You should record short videos about the work you do."

"But I have no experience..." I started to protest, but she quickly interrupted me. "You don't need experience," she said. "All you have to do is record what you do and put short fragments of your meetings up on YouTube. You will be surprised how many people will watch them." She then volunteered to organize and edit the recordings. I felt I could not refuse such a generous offer. I felt her services were heaven-sent and that without her I would continue working with individuals and small groups of people, without reaching the people I knew I was meant to reach.

That weekend I visited the Rubin Himalayan Museum. Full of artifacts from Tibet and Nepal, the museum has a room that has been decorated like a temple, with an altar and statues of the Buddha. The atmosphere in the little room, with its dim lights and burning incense, is conducive to meditation. Very few people linger there, so it is usually possible to spend some quiet time in contemplation and solitude.

I was thinking about the healing meeting I had hosted at the apartment a few days earlier and I realized that healing is a special gift, which appeared in our small gathering and, in fact, had attended me in my encounter with Mrs. Grey, as well as with other people throughout my life. It became clear to me that spontaneous healing had been happening around me for years, though I had never before credited my presence with healing powers. However, I now saw that healing had been a continuous theme throughout my life. I still did not want to take credit for these healings, because I knew that the healing force or energy is a universal gift, and, as I had told the people at the meeting, it comes when it wants to because it has its own intelligence.

So, if indeed I was a healer, what would be my next step? Should I put everything aside to develop my healing skills and help the sick and the needy for the rest of my life? I felt hesitant and I was not sure why that would be the case. Then, I heard a voice in my head and I was certain it was coming from one of the statues of the Buddha. What the voice told me was that my destiny was not to be a healer but to work tirelessly to educate people so that they might understand the worlds of energy and power and heal themselves.

"Big changes are coming to your planet," the statue said. "There need to be guides and teachers who can help people in the awakening process. Healing is just the first step toward wellness. Evolution, on the other hand, is about a quantum leap in consciousness. The one part of the human that is not fully evolved is the brain. The brain is an organ which is much more capable than is currently the case—you humans are only using a small fragment of your brain/mind capability.

"Evolution is coming to the human race. There are children being born today who are not only healers, but they are clairvoyant and wise beyond their years as well. You have probably heard of indigo children and crystal children. This next generation will see emerald children being born who will bring with them the ways and means to build a new Atlantis right here in the West."

When Tuesday came, I felt nervous. I had bought new mugs and tea; I had cleaned the apartment and borrowed a couple of chairs from my neighbor. It felt like a new beginning of something important—more like a mission than a small gathering of friends. Punctually at 8 P.M. the doorbell rang. It was Rosa. As soon as she came in and sat down, the doorbell rang again. For the next 15 minutes I was constantly running to the door as a new arrival would be expecting to be let in. By the time it was a quarter past eight there were 15 people sitting in my living room, seven of whom I had never met before. Friends had brought friends and it seemed that the word had spread—something exciting was going on on Second Avenue!

The first thing I did was to explain that I could no longer host such a large group of people in the little apartment, especially if it were to grow any further. Already every seat was occupied and people were sitting on the floor, so that there was virtually no room to move around in. People's bags and coats were piled up in the small bedroom and I wondered whether such a large gathering in such a small space represented a fire hazard.

Then something happened that assured me that I was in the right place at the right time. As all the visitors finally sat down and seemed to settle into place, I knew what I had to say. Perhaps it was channeling—connecting to an energy and knowledge from outside of myself. It felt like a "download," just like when you buy an application on the Internet and it gets transmitted to your computer in a matter of seconds. Or perhaps it was a distant memory of something I had heard before. Either way, I suddenly knew what to say.

"Today we are going to talk about the energy field that surrounds every human being. It is the shape of an egg and it pulsates and radiates with energy. If you stretch out your arms,"—people were lifting their arms and trying to stretch them out to the side without hitting their neighbor, which was difficult and in some cases impossible—"you are probably touching the edge of your aura. As you sit there, your energy fields are mingling with each other and you are creating a collective field between you. Every group which comes together forms such a field—some stronger than others. That is why it is sometimes difficult to disagree with a group of people or go against their collective aims and desires. A group energy is stronger than the sum of each individual's power."

"What about couples?" Mandy asked from the back of the room.

"People in a relationship form a field between them which grows in strength as the relationship builds and grows over time. There are many

In·sight: MOMENTS OF BEING

kinds of relationships and no two fields are the same. So in an abusive relationship one partner is taking energy from the other, causing the other person to lose energy, which can eventually lead to all kinds of difficulties, including divorce, disease or even death. In a good relationship, however, both partners become energized as they are able to draw in more energy into their mutual field, due to the energy exchange that happens between them. If you think of the various relationships in your life—past and present—I am sure that you can identify those that make or made you feel good about yourself, as well as those which were indifferent and those that caused you to feel defeated and depleted.

"When you go to hospital to visit a friend or a loved one, apart from the flowers or care package, you bring with you your energy and in a way which might even be unconscious you transmit energy to them, wishing them well. In that situation you don't mind that you feel tired and drained afterward, because you feel you have done a good deed and a useful service to your friend. But if you are in a relationship which tires you out, in the same way as you might feel tired after having visited a friend in hospital—you will soon begin to wonder whether you should continue being within such a relationship."

I looked at Mandy and I could see she was nodding her head. It was clear to me that she was thinking of her own history and experience.

"Energy is everywhere," I continued. "In your home, at the place where you work, in the shopping mall, down the street, everywhere. That is why you like to go to certain places and in other places you might feel uncomfortable. Yes, we like certain landscapes, colors and décor, but the energy is what affects us immediately as we enter a building or meet another person. Think of the many homes you have visited, even briefly. Which ones felt comfortable and energizing and which ones felt alien and hostile or just dirty and messy? Were there places where you felt you had to escape as soon as possible? And were there other homes or places where you felt you could stay for a long time and enjoy being there?"

A girl sitting on the floor in the front raised her hand.

"What's your name?" I asked.

"Flora," she replied.

"Yes, Flora."

"My uncle has a beautiful home," she said, "furnished with antiques and decorated with precious items from around the world, but every time I go there I feel uncomfortable and it feels like something is crawling all over my skin."

"That is the energy of the place," I replied. "You are very sensitive, Flora. There might be something either in the history of the house or in your uncle's life that is incompatible with your energy."

"My aunt—his wife—committed suicide two years ago," Flora said. A hush fell over the room and I could feel a change in the atmosphere as thoughts of a person killing themselves descended into the room.

"Can you feel that?" I asked. "Certain words are associated with different levels of energies. Flora's example introduced an energy that made us feel uncomfortable.

"I'm sorry," Flora said quietly as she lowered her eyes.

"Don't be," I said. "It's probably the best lesson we could all have had today. We all felt the collective energy that has been established among us change. If the level of energy can be lowered, it can also be raised.

"Let's talk for a moment about angels—human angels, that is. Have you ever met someone who has brought nothing but joy into your life? Someone who was there for you in your hour of need or helped you at a time of crisis and wanted nothing in return?"

Someone at the back raised their hand. It was Mandy's sister, Rosa.

"I was driving late at night in a deserted area and I punctured one of my tires. When I opened the trunk, I realized I didn't have a spare. I was standing at the side of the road, wondering what to do or who to call, when a car drove up, a man got out and quickly jacked the car up and effortlessly took the wheel off. He then drove off, saying, 'I'll be back' and, indeed, he was back within what felt like minutes with the fixed tire. He then put it back on and drove off before I could even thank him properly or offer to pay him."

"Thank you, Rosa. I believe that at any moment we are capable of connecting to any level of energy—high or low. But it is up to us and it is our human privilege of choice to decide what kinds of energies we want to collect within our field.

"I can see and feel your energy. You have exactly the same faculties and abilities as I do, only perhaps you have not been trained yet how to use them. As you become more sensitive, you too will be able to discern which energies are good for you and which places, people and circumstances it would be better for you to avoid."

A few hands went up and I could tell they wanted a personal reflection about their particular energy field.

"I do not do personal readings of people's energy field; I try not to pry into other people's lives. But I can't help seeing if someone is under a dark energy cloud composed of worry or disease. Yes, I can help a person get rid of their energetic wounds, especially if they are caused by past trauma or events that are no longer influencing their current feelings or thoughts. You see, emotions and thoughts are both energies that fill our auras every moment of every day. If you stretch out your hand in front of you, you are touching your energy field, which has many levels. As you then bring your hand closer to your chest, you might feel a wave of warmth—that is your energy emanating from your heart, which according to tradition and ancient sages is the seat of your emotions. If you now bring your hand to rest above your head"—they all raised their hands in the air—"you will feel the radiation emanating from your head which is the energy manufactured by your brain and thinking capability." I paused for a moment as people began sensing the different areas of their energy field.

"Wow," one of the young men in the second row exclaimed, "I can feel it. It's warm, almost like a dense stream of air."

"That's exactly right," I confirmed. "The top of your head is discharging energy all the time. It's like a little generator or furnace. It is very rare that we are able to quiet our thoughts and stop thinking, even for a moment. If trained, we can do it during meditation and we also tend to relax and let go of our thoughts during dreamless sleep."

I paused for a moment while the people in the room continued to sense the energy above their head and in front of their chest. Some even reached out and extended their hands into the energy field of the person they were sitting next to.

"In order to feel the energy and sensitize your hands," I continued, "bring your fingers together, as if you were going to collect water into the palms of your hands. There are several ways to wake up the nerve endings in the hands so they become more alert. You can simply close your fists and then open your palms several times, as if you were squeezing a soft ball or wet dishcloth." I demonstrated the action for all to see and they followed my example.

"The other exercise you can do is to simply clap your hands together." The room erupted with applause.

"But one thing to know about the sound of clapping is that it disperses an atmosphere. So once you begin sensing or meditating or healing, it is best not to clap. Have you noticed how sometimes after a powerful theatrical performance an audience is reluctant to clap and all hold still for a moment, not wishing to disperse the atmosphere that had been built by the actors? When you go to a performance of sacred dancing in India, they ask you to clap before the dance begins but not afterwards. That is because the whole purpose of the dance is to summon an energetic presence for the benefit of the audience. Conversely, during a Chinese New Year celebration there is much banging of cymbals and drums to disperse the energies of the old year and make room for the new."

"Does that mean that it would be a good idea to clap and make a noise when moving into a new apartment or house?" asked a woman sitting on the sofa.

"Absolutely," I replied. "How to energetically clear and clean a space is an ancient science; it is something that is usually done before a ceremony or ritual. That is why they use bells and incense in temples and churches all over the world. An atmosphere can be influenced both from the outside or the inside. Let me give some examples. If you are planning a romantic evening, you will play soft music, light candles and turn down the electric lights. You might decorate the room with flowers and spray the air with essential oils collected from flowers. All these actions will create an atmosphere that is conducive to intimate conversation and romantic feelings. If, on the other hand, you were to prepare for a religious ceremony, you might play a recording of Gregorian chants, burn some frankincense and add religious symbology to the ambience, like a crucifix or a statue of Buddha." I paused for a moment as the atmosphere in the room changed again.

"Can you feel that?" I asked. "You all thought of your experiences visiting a church, a synagogue or a temple and the atmosphere in the room changed. The atmosphere was influenced from the inside out. By mentally conjuring up an image of a place, you connected to its energy field and brought it here into the room. We could all feel that."

"For a moment it made me think I was in church," said a young girl sitting by the window.

"People create atmospheres by what they think," I confirmed. "That is why a gifted orator can cause audiences to both laugh and cry or to become inspired. He can also rally them to action. Incense, music, bells and candles can help, but only because of the associations created in the human mind. Your mind is a very powerful creator and master of energies—it can attract to itself what it wants and create alternative realities that energetically are just as real as the physical world we live in. When it allies itself with the emotions and a person's feelings, it virtually becomes unstoppable, drawing to itself people, situations and circumstances which are on the same frequency as the energies it had first created in the energy realms.

"Your mind is your reality. This is where you build your castles and create your future. You people it with your wishes and desires and the more you follow this energetically created world with actions, the more real it becomes. That is what the Law of Attraction is all about. Your mind

The Rubin Museum

can transform the fantasy and manifest it into reality, because it is able to pinpoint exactly where and how you can achieve your goals. That is why it is so important to have a mission and a vision, to go after what you want and to never give up. People who know what they want and are prepared to work for it, taking one step at a time and contributing to their dream every day are those who achieve their heart's desires. It might be the heart that desires, but it is the mind that finds a way to achieve it. The mind is the energetic life of the brain—the powerful field that can be either present or absent, as in the expressions 'mindless,' 'absent-minded,' or 'mindful.' The mind is your great ally, though it can also be a great preventer if it grows lazy and loses sight of the target."

"What about healing?" someone asked from the back. "Can the mind conquer disease?"

"Absolutely," I replied. "Medical miracles occur every day. Doctors can't explain it but sudden reversals are always possible. I have seen it myself," I added as I thought about Mrs. Grey. "That is why it is good to practice visualization so you can learn to attract to yourself what you want."

"Can you give an example?" Rosa persisted.

"Let's start with something simple," I said. "Close your eyes, take a deep breath and relax. Now imagine something you want. Keep it simple. It can be an object like a pair of shoes, a book or a day at the spa. Now imagine that you have it or that you are there. Visualize the feeling that would accompany achieving this one desire—touch it, sense it, smell it. Connect to its energy and let it surround you. Take a moment to be with it." I paused and as a hush descended upon the room, I could sense the energy associated with people's many wishes appearing within their energy fields.

A few minutes later I decided it was time for a tea break. I asked Mandy to help me and as we were preparing the tea in the kitchen, the doorbell rang. I answered the buzzer. It was Richard.

"I am so sorry about what happened," he said. "Can I come up and apologize in person?"

I thought for a moment, but decided it would be a good time to see him. "Come on up," I said. I think he was somewhat surprised to receive the invitation. A few moments later I opened the door and there he was. He could see Mandy passing from the kitchen to the living room with a tray of cups and mugs behind me.

"You have company," he hesitated.

"It's all right, come in," I said. He stepped across the threshold and I closed the door behind him. He bent over and whispered in my ear. "Ravens are people who cause trouble in your life," he said. "We mean no harm, but we do challenge your beliefs. As long as you know what you want, you have nothing to fear from a Raven." I didn't know whether to laugh or be angry with him, but I couldn't help but smile. I led him into the living room. He stopped in the doorway, again surprised by the number of people in the room. "This is Richard," I introduced him. A few people said "Hi" and Richard took a seat on the sofa, as a couple of people shifted to make room for him.

"Okay, let's start," I said. "We were talking about healing and visualization," I reminded the gathering. "Does anyone here have a headache?" I asked. A hand went up in the back. It was Mandy's boyfriend, Adam. I stood up and placed a chair in the middle of the ring of people.

"Come and sit in this chair," I said. Adam made his way to the middle of the room and sat down. "Adam's energy field comes out to about here," I demonstrated. I could feel the edge of his aura. "I am now sensing to see if I can detect any hot spots above his head." I raised my hand above his head. I then started bringing it closer in to the back of his head and I suddenly felt a wave of heat emanating from the back of his neck.

"Ouch," Adam said.

"I can feel heat," I said. I kept my hand there for a moment, then I gathered the heat into my hand and flicked it into a vase of flowers that was standing on a table nearby. "The energy that causes headaches in humans is food for plants," I explained. I repeated the same action three or four times.

"That feels better," said Adam. "It's like a weight has been lifted off my shoulders."

"Heat that gathers at the back of the neck is often caused by contradiction," I explained. I then asked Adam, "Have you been hesitating about something lately? Not sure about a decision you need to make?"

Adam turned toward me. "That's right," he said. "I've been offered a job but I am not sure whether to take it. Mandy wants me to, because it would pay well but I think I would be bored." Out of the corner of my eye I could see that Mandy, who was now sitting on the sofa next to Richard, was blushing.

"If you rearrange the letters in the word hesitations, it says 'it heats ions.' The back of the neck is where the brain in the head meets the spine. The nerves in your spine are like another brain. Someone who is spineless is a person who finds it difficult to say no. The brain in your head is the one that says yes. So when you vacillate between yes and no, there is a contradiction that builds up at the back of your neck and causes heat. That is why someone who is hesitating will often place his or her hand at the back of the neck to cool that area down. I have just taken away some of the static build-up from behind Adam's neck and he feels better already."

"The headache has gone," Adam confirmed. "What is more important is that I have made up my mind. I am not taking the job." A moment later he added, "I feel enveloped and protected, as if in a cocoon of energy."

"That is the healing energy," I said. "It has its own intelligence and mission. It comes when it wants to." I took a pause. "It is here," I said, as I could see a swirling green energy spiral around Adam. "Can you see it?" I asked. A few people gasped and a few more raised their hands. "It's green," an older man exclaimed. "I have never seen anything like it."

"The world is changing and becoming more charged. More and more people are seeing the realms of energy. Those who do are now seeing colors and shapes they had never seen before. We are living in a changing world and the veil between the seen and unseen is lifting."

A few more people confirmed that they could see a color around Adam. Even Richard was nodding.

In·sight: MOMENTS OF BEING

A young woman raised her hand. "I am a nurse," she said. "Can I do what you are doing and help our patients?"

"Of course you can," I said. "The healing energy does not belong to me or any one person. It is a universal visitor here. It comes through a person who is prepared to practice and learn, and keeps an open mind. The moment you think it is you doing the healing, it will go away."

Then something unexpected happened. Richard stood up and spoke, addressing the gathering. "This is a taste of the future," he said. "There is a new human genetic which is appearing here on Earth. It could be called *homo illuminatis* or *homo spiritualis*. It is a human who can see the worlds of energy and has the capability of being clairvoyant and prescient. I believe we all have the potential to become this new human and to develop our sensitivity and extra-sensory perception skills. This training that you are experiencing now could save your life in the future. The world needs healers. The Dalai Lama has said, and I quote, 'The world doesn't need more successful people; the world desperately needs more peacemakers, healers, restorers, storytellers and lovers of all kinds.' I believe you are these people. In the sixties we had the theme, 'Make love, not war.' Today it should be, 'Heal, don't harm.'"

I looked at Richard in surprise. I could now see the magician in him. Before my very eyes he had turned into a sincere and powerful teacher. I now saw him as a friend and ally.

"That's right," I confirmed. "We are embarking on a journey of development, within which we will be training to become the teachers and healers of the future."

Chapter Twenty-Two

Honor

When I got back to the apartment after work the next day I felt really tired. I took a shower, lay down on the bed and closed my eyes. I soon fell asleep and once again, I was back at the mystery school I had been at during the previous nights. This time the dream felt very real and by the time I woke up, I still was not sure whether I had been dreaming or whether the dream was real.

This time I dreamed I was in a large hall with a lot of other people, listening to a lecture. The Master was sitting on a dais and speaking to us about honor.

"It is often said of a person that they are a man or lady of honor. It usually means that they keep their word and fulfill their promises. According to novels about the time of chivalry, in those days the word was used much more often, to represent something deeper and more all-embracing. Honor represented a person's integrity, reliability, responsibility; it related to actions as well as words, and to motives as well as results. Thus a person of honor would be motivated by noble causes, championing the honor of ladies, defending the wronged, the under-privileged and the distressed.

"Today honor is a rare word, but in those few who recognize it and promote it, it refers to a way of life, where a person is guided by issues and aims greater than their personal gain or comfortability. To be honorable is to acknowledge that one is part of the human race and the planetary ecology and that one is responsible for its continuance and maintenance. It also suggests that one acknowledge one's part in Creation. It means being constant and true, not only to one's word, but to one's beliefs and motives. It will cause a person to keep one's side of the bargain, providing the bargain involves the benefit of both sides, also encompassing the idea of human and planetary evolution.

"Honor looks to the future as well as accepting the past. It deals with what is without bias, fantasy or wishful thinking.

"Why is a judge referred to as 'Your Honor' in Britain? Because a judge was meant to embody the quality of honor in an unbiased, impartial and just way. Members of Parliament are meant to be *honorable* and with that comes a lack of self-interest and a genuine concern for the greater 'interest'—of the country, the people, the planet and the universe.

"Think of the expression *keeping one's word*. What would the opposite of that be? Giving it away? Wasting it? Abandoning it? Keeping one's word speaks of a constancy and a consistency. For what does one keep? Those things that are precious, meaningful and of value. In old castles the keep was the enclosure in the middle of the fortifications where precious jewels and treasures were preserved in safety.

"There is another phase, i.e. *my word is my bond*. In both these sayings it is implied that a person does what they say they will do; they fulfill their promises. What is it like to deal with a person who does this? You come to rely on their words, you take them seriously and you know that they won't let you down. If you want the respect of others, then all you need to do is to become such a person. And one way to become such a person is not to promise anything lightly, but always think whether you can fulfill a promise before you make it. Saying 'Yes' is easy, but carrying out that commitment might not be. Learn to be realistic and to think through with care each promise, taking into account all ramifications and consequences.

"Keeping your word also means remembering it, knowing what you had said to whom and when. It means keeping it current until it is fulfilled

Honor

and dispatched.

"What is it like to deal with a person who does not fulfill their promises? At first there is disappointment, and then you learn not to trust them any more and not to believe a word they say. How can anything valuable or lasting be built upon such a relationship? It is an impossibility.

"Honor is the foundation upon which true relationships are built. Love and honor belong together, like two twin sisters. Adopt both these energies into your energy field and you will be glad—it will open you up to real, caring relationships and it will demonstrate to other people that you are an honest, reliable and trustworthy person."

Chapter Twenty-Three

Imagine

The next time I met the group (in my mind I was referring to them as "the group") we gathered at the Imagine area in Central Park. The sun was shining brightly and there was no one else in the vicinity to disturb the feeling of quiet and tranquility during this late summer afternoon. We stood together and closed our eyes, trying to sense the energy field created by the group, but making sure we were not inventing into what we thought we felt.

I was not aware of any particular image, but could distinctly feel a blue mist enveloping the group as it brought with it a sense of calm and settlement. My sense was confirmed by Mandy, who was fast becoming one of the more sensitive members of our gathering.

"I feel so peaceful," she said. "I could just stand here for hours."

"I asked everyone to meet me here because this area in Central Park is dedicated to the memory of John Lennon, who, as you know, was murdered very close to here, in front of the Dakota building at 1 West 72nd Street where he lived. It is also dedicated to John Lennon's song, *Imagine* and the power of the imagination. Never underestimate the power of your imagination and always remember to dream big. Know what you want and picture it in your mind—make it real. But don't just dream for yourself—dream for others, dream for the country, dream for the human race. John

In·sight: MOMENTS OF BEING

Lennon's song spoke of all people living life as one. That dream still seems a long way off, but I do believe it is coming. By adding our dreams to the greater dream for peace and unity among all people, we are strengthening that dream, adding our power to it and bringing it just a little bit closer.

"The religions of the world disagree on many issues, and they follow the teachings of different prophets, and adhere to different sacred writings. But there can be only one truth. All major religions were born in the past—they fulfilled a role for the times and places where they first emerged. But today planet Earth has moved on to a different part of the universe; the energy from the stars, planets and the cosmos that is bombarding this planet at this very moment has changed and has evolved. We, too, are evolving and developing new sensitivities to the energy worlds. The fact that you are here and can feel this new energy proves it. But the old is still holding on to the past and it is just this conflict between the two—the old and the new—that we are born into. We are the children of the cusp—born between the ages of Pisces and Aquarius—and we are the people who carry the responsibility for the future. It is down to us to lead and teach others—to become healers and the educators for these times. Look around you at this group of misfits who did not fit into any traditional mold—we are feeling the change as this new Age of Aquarius is taking hold and transforming our ability to imagine the future."

As I was speaking, I could feel a spinning sensation in my head. I looked around me and I could see a blue mist once again descending over the gathering. Some passers-by had joined the growing crowd and everyone was listening attentively.

"Can you see it?" I asked and several people confirmed that they could see the blue mist. It felt cool and calming despite the hot weather.

"There is a healing presence here," I said. "Whenever there is a new religious or spiritual presence that periodically comes to planet Earth and brings with it an evolutionary upgrade to the human race, it is accompanied by a healing entity. All the great prophets and those connected to high universal energies were also healers. However, today we do not await a single prophet or guru to show us the way; we do not expect the next sacred book to be dictated by an angel. It is up to us to write the future and become the healers, by first healing ourselves. So take this blue mist with you and let it heal you and guide you as we continue to imagine a future without famine or war."

I took a deep breath and paused. I looked into the sky and high above the crowd I saw a whole swarm of birds fly overhead. They filled the whole sky and seemed to be circling around us. Everyone else also looked to the sky and I could hear gasps of awe and amazement.

"The birds are attracted by the healing angel that is present here today. Birds are very sensitive to energies and will respond to high essences when they are present."

I then had a very real sense of the dangers facing those who are audacious enough to challenge the status quo and to bring new energies and new beliefs to the planet, influencing social orders and altering political systems.

"Every time there is an opportunity for human evolution and for a new belief system to become established in the world, there will be those who oppose the threat to their established power and superior position in the world. So beware of those who will hate you and will want to annihilate you and destroy your work. Just like Mark David Chapman shot John Lennon, so will you develop enemies, if you wish to continue on this path of human evolution and change. For every action there is an equal and opposite reaction. Sometimes you can best measure the power of a thought or a deed by gauging the opposition to it. So be brave and be dedicated because change is coming, whether there are people in the world who like it or not and whether we will become those people who help implement it or not."

Chapter Twenty-Four

Love

That night during my astral travels the Master appeared before me as I stood in the large meeting hall, surrounded by other acolytes who, like me, had just gathered for a meeting.

"The highest quality you can aspire to while alive on planet Earth is love. But there is no quality that provokes more misunderstanding and abuse than love. 'I love you' are words that can so easily roll off your tongue. However, real love is not common—it's pure and unique and if it has any possession attached to it at all, it is no longer love.

"If you reverse the word love to *evol*—these are the first letters of the words evolve or evolution. To love something or someone is to want it to evolve and be the best it can be. If you want something or someone to stay the same—either out of convenience or habit—then you are being possessive, not loving.

"Possession does not come from the heart, but love does. It radiates with a warm glow that supports and nourishes all within its sphere of influence. It is maternal by nature, for does the mother not love her children selflessly and work tirelessly, providing them with nourishment, warmth and sharing her knowledge with them as they learn and grow? Which mother does not want her children to grow into strong, healthy, responsible and wise human beings? And yes, there might be exceptions to this statement,

In·sight: MOMENTS OF BEING

but I am talking about natural motherhood and the maternal instinct that most mothers experience and embody.

"There are people who claim they love someone, but if their love is unrequited, it can so easily turn to hatred. This is not love; it is possession.

"So, your tasking today is to find examples of love—real people, real love. Listen carefully and find out how people use that word. If you do, you might be able to identify the different levels of love."

I had no idea where to start so I decided to go for a walk in the garden to collect my thoughts and work out what to do to fulfill my tasking for the day. As I walked past the greenhouse, I noticed through the glass that one of the gardeners was busy repotting some lilies. He waved at me as I walked by, so I decided to go into the greenhouse and tell him how beautiful I thought the flowers in his care were.

"Those are beautiful," I said, approaching the bench at which he was working.

"They really are," he confirmed. "I love lilies. I don't think you will be able to find any lilies more beautiful than these." He lovingly touched one of the flowers with his fingers. "As you can see, they come in all colors—pink, orange, white, yellow and lilac. Just look at this tiger lily here," he said, pointing to a beautiful orange specimen with white edges on its petals and black dots near the middle of the flower. "I have developed this one myself," he said with pride.

"They are indeed beautiful," I confirmed again. "And this one is like the queen of all lilies."

"Funny you say that," the gardener smiled at me. "I called it the Royal Tiger."

"It's a very appropriate name," I said. "Thank you," I added, as I turned to leave.

As I left the greenhouse, I realized I had my first example of love—a gardener who loved his plants. But was this real love? And if so, how could I describe it? I was thinking about it when I noticed a girl and her dog walking toward me. As we were about to pass each other, the dog suddenly veered to one side and ran a circle around me, entangling me in his leash. Both the girl and I came to a stop next to each other as we tried to release me from the entanglement.

"So sorry," said the girl. "I do apologize." She was clearly embarrassed. "They don't know what they are doing. He obviously liked you," she added, as she loosened the grip of the leash and I was able to step out of my imprisonment.

"It's okay," I said, smiling. The dog was wagging his tail like crazy. The girl picked the dog up and held him in her arms, as if he were a baby.

"You've got to love them," she said as she kissed the dog lightly on its nose. "They are so lovable."

"He is very cute," I confirmed. "Bye," I added as I walked away. Here was that word again. One can love flowers, dogs, just about anything. As if to confirm my thoughts, my next encounter was with a young child walking with her mother. She was skipping along holding an ice cream cone. As we passed, I could hear her say, "I love ice cream! Specially pistachio." She clearly had a bit of trouble saying the word *pistachio*, and it came out more like *pissed acho*. I smiled to myself as I walked by, thinking about love. It occurred to me that in the case of loving ice cream, or strawberries, or any food, one could substitute the word *love* with *like*. So at one level love meant *to like a lot, to have a profound fondness for*.

So what about loving another person? I felt there was a lot more to discover about love. I walked back to the school building and headed into the dining room. There were several people sitting at the tables, drinking coffee or tea and having conversations about the work they were engaged in. I spotted a young woman who was sitting on her own. I poured myself a cup of tea from the large urn that was always available to the students and headed in her direction.

"Can I join you?" I asked.

"Sure," she said as she waved her arm in the direction of the chair on the other side of the table. I sat down.

"Thank you," I said. Before I had a chance to say anything else, she began to speak. "I was thinking about my boyfriend," she said. "I miss him so much," she added as she took a sip from her cup.

"Where is he?" I asked.

"He is in China," she replied. "He will be there for two more months. He is away on an archeological field trip."

"Do you love him?" I asked, thinking that here I might have an example of a higher form of love than any of the previous examples I had seen so far.

"Of course I love him," the woman said. "What is there not to love? He is good to me and he is a good provider. He is a keeper. Of course I love him," she repeated, and it sounded as if she was trying to convince herself about it.

I finished my tea and thanked the woman for her company. I walked out of the building and started walking toward the nearby village. Surprisingly, that afternoon I came across yet another form of love as I came closer to the main street where all the shops and restaurants were. A car pulled up to the curb as I was walking by and an old man came out of the car on the driver's side. He walked around to the other side of the car and opened the passenger's door. He then proceeded to help an older woman get out of the car. The woman had a cast on one of her legs. While the man was supporting her and as she leaned against him, he reached into the back seat of the car and retrieved a pair of crutches. When he tried to close the car door, one of the crutches slipped out of his hand and fell to the ground. The man handed the other crutch to the woman while I bent over, picked up the crutch that was lying in the gutter and handed it to the woman. The woman had now freed herself from the man's embrace and took the other crutch from me as she steadied herself on one leg.

"Thank you," she said as she supported herself between the two crutches. "You have been most helpful." I smiled. She continued to speak. "He does everything for me," she said. "We have been together now for over forty years and he still treats me like a princess."

"Oh, don't exaggerate, Martha," the man said. "It is simply what any decent husband would do."

The woman smiled. "Decent being the operative word," she said, as they slowly walked together toward the doctor's office a few doors away—she on her crutches and he watchful, making sure she was all right.

"I do love the way you won't take credit for all the years of devotion," I heard her say to him as they disappeared out of earshot.

That evening the Master asked me to join him in the garden. He was sitting on a bench next to a small fountain and he invited me to sit down beside him.

"So you have learned about love today," he initiated the conversation.

"Yes, I have," I confirmed. "There seem to be many meanings to the word *love*—we can love our food, our pets or plants or other people. If we love other people it can be because of what they can do for us or because of who they are and the time and experiences we have shared with them."

"Yes, but there is also a higher form of love," the Master said. "It encompasses all and has no judgment or conditions. The words *unconditional love* have been overused and misused but the real word for unconditional love is *compassion* because it encompasses all. Like a compass that is used to draw a complete circle, compassion encircles all within its sphere and influence. You will do well to learn about compassion, which is the highest form of love," he added.

Chapter Twenty-Five

Love, New York

Facing a large crowd in front of the sculpture dedicated to love in New York City, I realized that while I was trying to be in service and searching for my next calling, it had found me and I had become a teacher. I had never intended to instruct others, but I always wanted to learn. I understood that that was precisely what this life was for, at least for me. The best way to learn is to teach. I used to think that a teacher was someone who knew best and no longer needed to study or improve. How wrong I had been! Perfection on planet Earth is not an option. However, striving for perfection is.

I wonder if somewhere in the universe there is a perfect planet with perfect people living perfect lives. Surely not, for the universe itself is expanding and growing every day. We are made in the image of the universe, so we have the option to expand and grow as well.

I looked out at the sea of faces—all colors, all ages, all shapes, all sizes. The message about the gathering had gone viral and there were now hundreds, if not thousands of people filling up the Avenue of the Americas, disrupting the traffic and bringing both cars and pedestrians to a halt. I was standing in front of an imperfect crowd, all striving for perfection in their own way and all hoping for words of wisdom that would bring them closer to the truth—their truth, my truth, universal truth. All I could offer them was an understanding about the energy that I felt was arriving from the universe that very moment—not a previously written lesson and not a rehearsed idea or action. I suddenly understood that I needed to trust the universal teacher, the guide within, the eternal spirit that has access to all knowledge of all times.

"We are blessed," I said, and it felt as if it was the voice of someone else, perhaps an ancient ancestor or a future child, speaking, "for we are not perfect. Always we have something to strive for. And it is this striving, this incessant urge to improve, to discover, to do more, that brings happiness and elevates us above the beasts of the field. We might have many ambitions and want to achieve this or that—be rich, famous or loved. But once accomplished, each goal can become a disappointment if we do not use it as a foundation for the next target. So do not become attached to your achievements, for they are only staging posts on the way. You have no idea who you can become, so do not limit yourself with your ideas of who or what you want to be. The future is unwritten, so do not fill in the blanks too early. Aim high but do not become disappointed if your dreams are not fulfilled the way you would wish them to be or within the time frame you have given yourself.

"The universe might have other plans for you, so listen to that inner voice that will guide you if you give it a chance to speak to you. You can never know all the ingredients that come together to shape your future—you can only estimate what you think might be possible for you. Allow yourself the freedom to think big and outside the box and to reinvent yourself whenever you feel the time is right. From this moment on there are a thousand futures awaiting you and it is for you to choose which path you will adopt as your own. You have only one past and one present, but your freedom lies in your multiple futures, within which you can choose to be whoever you want to be."

I paused for a moment. I felt I was instructing myself and listening to the words even as they were leaving my mouth and reaching over the gathering. At that moment I realized with certainty that there was a new age dawning and that there was a new energy entering the planet, transforming minds and hearts and opening people's perception to the idea of further evolution. The human story was not about to end—it was just beginning and we were witnessing a wave of some very refined energy that was enveloping us all in a feeling of wonder. I noticed that the light in the street changed and there was an illumination that seemed to come from deep within each person who was there. It became tinged with a light blue mist that reminded me of the blue mist that had appeared when we had gathered at the Imagine memorial only a few weeks before.

At that moment I knew this was just the beginning and we were starting a world movement. It was at that moment that a shot ran out, I felt a sudden pain and then everything went dark as I could feel myself falling, falling, falling...

Chapter Twenty-Six

Trust

It was my last day at the mystery school and my last test and it was going to be a ceremonial event. I was led into a great hall that I had never been in before—there was a large platform surrounded by tiered seating, as in an amphitheater. The room was flanked by large columns and arches and with a domed ceiling overhead. There were many people in the hall—standing or seated, talking, conversing, meditating or praying. They were all dressed in long white robes, as if they had just arrived from the ancient world or from a Middle Eastern desert. I was led onto the platform and immediately the conversations ceased and the voices hushed. I knew this was an important moment and that if I were to pass this test, my life would never be the same again.

Suddenly two great wooden doors opened and the Master entered, followed by a man carrying a silver platter on which were two silver goblets. The Master entered the platform and gestured to the man following him to wait outside the perimeter of the dais. He then addressed me in a voice loud enough for everyone to hear, "We have gathered together to witness your last task. All these people that you see have already been through a similar course and have now formed the Brotherhood of Humanity. This is the most difficult tasking of all."

He addressed the man with the platter and said, "Enter, brother

Matthew." Matthew entered the platform and stood silently a few steps away.

"There are two cups and they both contain a liquid. It is for you to choose to drink from one of them. But choose carefully. One of these cups might contain a deadly poison and the other does not. If you choose the wrong cup, you could be dead within minutes. It is your decision," said Brother Matthew.

I stepped back in horror. Poison? How could the Master offer me poison? Everything I had learned so far had been about living, about preserving the sanctity of life, about respecting oneself and others, about working with God and nature, not against them. I turned away and was ready to flee. I didn't want to be there; everything that had happened so far suddenly seemed to be a lie. This did not feel right. Who were these brothers and sisters anyway? I had heard that they were the Watchers and that their mission was to do good in the world, to share their knowledge, to promote peace and encourage quality wherever they found it. Slowly I looked around—I could see faces of all races and ages—so many different faces. They all had a certain gentleness about them, a knowing kindness and a firm encouragement.

I stood there for a moment, registering how I felt and I suddenly realized that I had initially reacted emotionally; I had allowed myself to get upset without thinking this through. For would they really want to kill someone they had been training for a long time to do God's work? Had they really gathered to watch the death of a neophyte? Had I had any indication at all that this was a doomsday cult or a black magic coven of witches or a group of Satan worshippers? I shuddered at the thought and quickly dismissed it from my mind. No, like all the other tests I now remembered I had been exposed to, this was a test of character. They wanted to know what was inside me and whether I had gathered to myself enough of holy energetic substances that would allow me to go into the world and represent them. I certainly could not very well represent them or myself or God or the universe if I was dead. Also, Brother Matthew did not say the cup contained poison, he explicitly suggested that it might be poisonous. I smiled to myself, for the thought of anyone wanting to poison me now seemed so ridiculous.

I took a step forward and peered into the cups which were still being held by Matthew. Both contained a clear liquid and both looked exactly the same.

I thought I understood at last. I was to use my sensitivity and discern which one contained the elixir. They were testing whether I could tell which was which. I sniffed the liquid, but to my nostrils and sense of smell they both seemed exactly the same. I stretched out my hand and held it over both cups. They felt the same—the air above both was cool and fresh and it felt like holding my hand over a stream on a hot summer's day. If one of them did indeed contain poison, I could not feel it and I could not imagine that they would let me drink it. Perhaps they were waiting for me to reach out for one of the cups, to make a choice, and if I made a mistake and reached for the wrong one, perhaps they would step in and prevent me from drinking it. I found this last thought reassuring and somewhat settling. This was, after all, a test and I had come through all the other tests unscathed and unhurt, but wiser and more experienced. How could it be that this test would be different? If it were poison, and if I chose it and if they really would watch me die, then I didn't want their training or their living or their tasks anyway. Therefore I could not lose. At that moment I suddenly realized that I had been dreaming and that in the hours of the night no harm could come to me anyway.

I looked at the Master who had accompanied me on my journey every step of the way; I looked into his eyes and saw the compassion and humility to a depth that I had not seen before in any other person's eyes. How could this man betray me? If this were possible then there was absolutely nothing in this world that I could trust anymore, including the evidence of my own senses and reason. I kept looking at him as I reached for one of the cups. It didn't matter which. As I brought the cup to my lips, I suddenly knew with the whole of myself that this was yet another test and that there was no poison, because there couldn't be.

The Master stepped forward and smiled. I seemed to recognize that smile, which radiated warmth and compassion.

"Brother Matthew was teasing you. We would never offer poison to another person, no matter who or what that person was," he said. "But his untimely joke has allowed us to observe your reaction and the many emotions and thoughts that fleetingly took residence upon your face and within your mind. You can safely choose which goblet you wish to drink from," he added with encouragement.

So with a fleeting smile, I drank from the cup, all the time looking into the Master's eyes. He did not move or flinch or smile. He just stood there, like a rock. But as soon as I started drinking, all the witnesses stood up to watch, very quietly and very intensely. By the time I had finished, they were all standing. I replaced the cup onto the tray and for a moment there was a deadly hush, as if everyone was waiting for something. But I already knew—I had chosen life. There was no need to examine the taste left in my mouth or to wait for odd symptoms. All I had done was to drink a cup of water. In the hush and the mounting expectation I reached for the second cup and as everyone seemed to hold their breath, I drank from that cup too, this time with firmness and certainty.

As I replaced the cup on the platter, several things happened all at once. Matthew silently withdrew from the platform, the Master approached me with a smile and embraced me and everyone all around started to cheer. There was such a noise that I thought the entire neighborhood would be woken up for miles around. And then, suddenly, all went quiet. The Master held me at arms length and said, "You have passed the most difficult test of all, which is the test of trust. I see that you have learned well and that you did not allow yourself to be governed by your emotions, but that you had made the attempt to look at our history together and from that to add up your present predicament. Well done. Mostly humans learn not to trust, but you have shown that trust is still possible. Use it wisely, for the world can be a dangerous place and trust is like a delicate flower that needs cultivation and care. You have found those that you can trust because you know how we think and why. Treasure this gift, for it will give you strength and sustenance in times to come."

There was another cheer and I began to feel embarrassed and self-conscious. But there was more to come. In the final part of the ceremony, I was led among the tiered seating and introduced to every member of the brotherhood I was about to join.

After the ceremony the Master explained to me that I had reached the next stage of my journey. "Now that you have shown that you trust me, from now on you will be connected to me and to that delicate stream of universal energy that is sent here by the wise beings that watch over this planet and support human evolution. You can now go into the world and teach what you have learned here.

"You are now an eagle. Go and fly free and bring messages from the universe to the people you teach. Just as in many churches sermons are read from a lectern in the shape of an eagle to symbolize God's words, so you are now the link between the higher and the lower energy realms, between heaven and Earth. Anyone can aspire to your status, but it takes time, diligence, discipline and an insatiable curiosity about everything to achieve it. You have also shown that you care about other people, the planet and life itself. From now on this is your sacred duty—to promote life wherever you find it and to protect it from evil."

He then bowed to me and I bowed in return. As I turned around to leave through the entrance to the school building, to go out into the world and fulfill my destiny, I noticed Henry among those watching. I smiled at him and he stepped forward.

"Did you know that Adler in German means eagle?" he asked.

"No, I had no idea," I replied as I took his arm and headed out toward the exit.

In·tuition

MOMENTS OF AWAKENING

In-Tuition; Moments of Awakening is the second of the three-part series of books, tracing the adventures of a young woman in search of meaning in her life.

To give the reader an opportunity to flavor Barbara's previous adventure at the mystery school where she meets the Master and continues her personal development journey, we attach the first chapter of this book for your reading pleasure.

Part one of the trilogy, *In-Formation: Moments of Realization* as well as part two of the trilogy, *In-Tuition: Moments of Awakening* are both available from major online booksellers, such as: www.Amazon.com and www.BarnesandNoble.com.

Chapter One
The Discovery

I really didn't mean to know. I wished I could reverse the onslaught of time and be ignorant again. I have no idea what caused me to put my hand into his jacket pocket as I took his suit to the cleaners. I never look through his pockets; it's the kind of thing you read about in novels, but if two people trust each other, you don't need to… Who am I kidding? I would so much like to think of myself as a sophisticated wife, secure and happy, trusting and loving. But suddenly all that wishful thinking was shattered in one brief moment as I stood in front of the counter and the lady asked me whether I wanted to check the pockets before I left the suit to be cleaned. It wasn't even my idea, as if the whole thing was a terrible joke played out by fate and everyone else, while I remained like a puppet, whose strings were being pulled by some invisible hands.

So there I was, jacket in one hand and that dreaded hotel bill in the other—I must have been quite a sight, seeing my name on a bill—Mr. and Mrs. Johnson—for a room at a place I had never been to. My mind was racing—September sixth, what day of the week was that? I couldn't think. I put the jacket back on the counter, took the receipt, even managed a smile and a "thank you" and dashed out of the door. I almost ran to the car, let myself in, threw my bag onto the passenger's seat and sat there, slowly gathering my thoughts, resting the bill in front of my eyes, using the steering wheel as a pulpit.

I didn't want to know on the one hand and I could have easily torn up the offending piece of paper and thrown it out of the window, pretending that this was not really happening. But there was also a great curiosity to know more. Who is she? Where did they go? What was the name of that hotel? were questions that were rattling around in my head, demanding answers. I carefully scrutinized the bill—The Golden Dusk Hotel. Hotel. Never heard of it. Certainly not a major chain or group of hotels. In a way that was a relief; it wasn't somewhere where we had been together, say for dinner or afternoon tea. And even as I looked, I was playing out scenarios in my head: The Confrontation and The Questioning. This was a drama with tragic-comic undertones with the final result being separation and divorce. Then there was the Playing Ignorance spy-thriller, trying to find out more, hiding around corners, opening letters, searching drawers and pockets for more evidence.

Mr. and Mrs. Johnson at the Golden Dusk Hotel—one night, breakfast and two phone calls. Even the phone numbers were on the bill. One was our home—he had phoned home—and one was to the office. Both numbers were so familiar to me, probably etched in my memory forever. The date—September sixth. When was that? I couldn't think; it was more than six weeks ago. It couldn't have been a weekend; I could account for every one of them. My mind was racing. I had a small diary in my bag—I pulled it out. Dentist appointment—that was the first thing I noticed about Wednesday, September sixth. Then, in small letters it said underneath: Andrew away at conference. The same writing appeared within the box for the previous Monday and Tuesday as well. A three-day conference. He was away for three days. That's right! I remembered now. I sighed and leaned back in the seat, as floods of memories from those three days rushed in. I could clearly see little snapshots of life at home, the things I did during those three days. And then I pictured the faces of his colleagues, the ones that I knew, who were supposed to have gone too. And then the one thing I did not want to submit to came in as an avalanche of doubt and suspicion:

The Discovery

Who was he with? Who could it be? In my mind's eye I searched a gallery of portraits—faces of friends, people we knew, people we met. Women, friends, colleagues. It was useless; I didn't know. It could be anybody; it shouldn't be anybody. Who knows how a man thinks? Sitting there was not going to solve anything. I needed to think this through. I needed to talk to somebody. I needed time.

I started the car and slowly drove toward home. I took my time as I tried to gather my thoughts. There were so many things I wanted to do—I wanted to run away, to confront him, to hire a detective to follow him and then I wanted to forget all those ideas and do nothing at all, to pretend nothing was happening so that life could carry on as before. But, of course, I knew it couldn't. I knew it never would be the same again.

When I got home, the house felt empty. I paced around the place, checking messages, making myself a cup of tea. I couldn't sit still, I didn't know what to do. As always, when at loss, I dialed Anne's familiar number. She was home. She answered the phone. Now what do I say? She picked up that something was wrong. After all, we knew each other well.

"Are you all right?" she asked.

Tears flooded to my eyes, as I answered, "No, I'm not. Can I come over?"

She always liked a good drama. "Sure," she said, "come right away."

On my way over to Anne's house I became subject to two mental processes, both related to and dependent on each other. The first was a great value and appreciation for the normality of things, and a further longing for life to be boring, mundane, uneventful, continuous and secure. I also felt the beginning of a realization that all that had now changed and that nothing would be the same ever again. I couldn't even begin to think about the future, for my whole life, as I knew it, stood in front of me now in ruins and I had no idea how to go about repairing it.

Then, in my desperate quest for some sort of solace or comfort, I found my mind racing through the various books I had read and films I had seen, in search of a similar scenario. I was sure this was a stereotype situation, very banal and a veritable template for many cheap paperback stories, which I used to consume voraciously when I was a teenager. And yet, for the life of me, I couldn't remember what ought to happen next according to any one of them. And then, suddenly, I remembered and it almost caused me to stop the car in the middle of the traffic. Of course, the wife doesn't find out till later, but it is always her best friend who is having an affair with her husband! Of course, Anne! How could I have not spotted it before? I'm going over to her place to pour my heart out and she will be mocking me because she already knows all about it. No doubt she will then urge me to get a divorce so she can have him all to herself! I quickly scanned in my mind all the times we had been out together, the three of us, and how well Anne and Andrew used to get on, how pleased I was and relieved that both of my favorite people enjoyed each other's company. What a fool I had been.

And then a further thought came into my head and that was that perhaps the hotel bill was left in his pocket on purpose, so that I would find it, demand an explanation and file for a divorce. Perhaps it was part of a plan, all thought out and premeditated to place the ball in my court, for me to make the decisions. Perhaps not completely consciously, but as part of a plan nevertheless.

In the meantime, I was nearing Anne's home and I needed to decide what I was going to tell her, how I would be with her and what would I give her the satisfaction of hearing. Before I had time to really think about it, I was parked outside her house and before I even had time to lock the car, she was standing in the doorway waiting for me to reach her at the top of the porch steps. As I walked toward her, I could see that she knew right away that something was the matter—she knew me too well. There was no point in pretending any more. I didn't want to anyway; I needed to talk to someone. And if it was her, then she would need to deal with her own guilt and decide whether she would be honest with me or not. I didn't care any more. It needed to come out into the open.

Anne put the kettle on to make tea, as she always did when I visited her. As soon as we sat down together in her living room, she asked, "What

The Discovery

is the matter?"

I immediately blurted out, to my own surprise as well as hers, "Andrew is having an affair!"

"Really?" she sounded genuinely surprised, but not shocked, and the next thing she asked was, "How do you know?"

So before I knew it, I was telling her the whole story, which wasn't much of a story, really, for all there was to report was the discovery at the dry cleaner's and that's it, with a few more speculations, indignations, surprises and bewilderments on my part. She seemed very sympathetic and quiet, with a few questions that I had already thought about, like, "When looking back, isn't there anything else you can see that now seems suspicious? Like unexpected business trips or unexplained expenses?"

Well, sure there was, but that's the way Andrew was anyway and that was the nature of his job—traveling a lot, spending generously during his trips and then claiming back expenses—it was all very difficult to keep track of. Money in, money out. I always saw myself as the policeman standing in the middle of a busy crossroads, directing the traffic, but never holding on to much in the process and never really investigating where the traffic was coming from or where it was going. As long as it was there, I had places to send it; as long as I could pay the bills and the mortgage for the next month, I trusted that the next bit would come in somehow so that we could continue. And so far it always did.

"Nothing more unexpected than usual," I replied, thinking hard, but not able to relate to anything suspicious or out of the ordinary, like an exotic perfume or unfamiliar scent.

"What about the classic one, lipstick on his collar?" Anne said, pouring another cup of tea. I couldn't control it and despite my grief and confusion, I burst out laughing.

"Oh, please," I said, indignant, though I knew I had no right to be after what had happened so far. "He would never do that."

"That's what every wife in your situation always says. But it does happen because it's one way of letting you know," Anne said, now turning into a psychologist. I could almost see her in a white coat with a pad and pencil in her hand. "Another, of course, is to leave a hotel bill in his coat pocket."

This thought took me by surprise. Not because I hadn't thought of that already—because I had—but because I didn't expect her to come up with it. I pretended to be ignorant or naïve or both.

"Are you saying that he did it deliberately?"

"Well, not necessarily consciously or deliberately," Anne explained, obviously pleased that I was taking her seriously. "But something in him wanted you to know, otherwise he would not have left that bill there. I believe," she added, with an air of authority, "that if someone wants to do something but doesn't know how and hesitates for too long, then their subconscious mind will find the opportunity to do it on its terms, whether the person agrees to those terms or not."

"Oh, Anne, you mean he wanted me to know so that I would take the initiative and walk away from our relationship? Or perhaps decide that I can forgive him and carry on? Is it that he can no longer live with the lie and the guilt?" I did not wait for an answer to all these questions that were spilling out, one after the other. "So what should I do? What would you do in my situation?" I asked rather pathetically, putting myself hypothetically in her care, sipping the comforting warm liquid in this otherwise unfamiliar new territory.

"I don't know," she hesitated. "What do you want to do?" she asked, emphasizing the word 'you.' And when I hesitated, taking a moment to reply, she continued, "I see three options here, depending upon what you want and what you are prepared to live with, or not prepared to live with, as the case may be. First, and the most dramatic, is to move out and file for divorce right away. The other extreme is to ignore the whole thing and carry on as if nothing has ever happened. But I don't think you would want to do that," she added, with a hesitation in her voice. "The third possibility is to confront him, talk it through and see if you can work something out, providing, of course, you both want to and are able to, after what has happened."

She's right, I thought. That leaves me two options: to say something or to shut up. Well, I knew that all along. I didn't need her to tell me that! Suddenly I felt resentful. How come she is so ordered and well organized, pontificating about what to best do? I thought and my suspicions grew stronger than ever. I started to feel like a hypocrite, sitting there with these accusatory thoughts knocking about in my head. I felt I had better leave.

"You're right," I said out loud to her. "It's simple, really. I just need to think it through and make a decision. Thanks for the tea." I stood up. My change of mood must have seemed abrupt to her.

"Where are you going?" she asked, responding to the sudden haste.

"I must get home. Just look at the time!" I said, glancing at my watch. It wasn't late at all and I knew Andrew wouldn't be home for some hours. If only I could listen in to her telephone conversations the moment I walked out the door. I felt sure she would be phoning him immediately to warn the perpetrator that they had been found out. We kissed on both cheeks, as we always did and said our goodbyes. I noticed her perfume—expensive, no doubt.

Back in the car, I dialed Andrew's office. "I'll put you through," said the receptionist and immediately I could hear the busy signal. The receptionist's voice came back on. "His line is busy. Do you want me to put you through to his voice mail?"

"No, it's all right, Anita. I'll talk to him later."

There it was—another proof, another piece of evidence. All right, I would take it all the way. I stopped the car and looked up the hotel on the Internet—the Golden Dusk. I phoned their office and asked for the address of the hotel. I was going to get to the bottom of this. Once I had the address, I worked out that it would take me about an hour to get there. I still had enough time to drive there and back before Andrew would come home. I dropped in to the house on my way and rummaged around in the box of photographs, where I found a picture of Andrew, Anne, Nick (Anne's current boyfriend at the time) and me, taken during last year's vacation in France. There we were in a vineyard in Provênce, tasting the grapes. How sun tanned and happy we all looked! How ironic! But it was a good, close up shot and you could clearly see Anne's features on it.

It didn't take me long to get out of town and the hotel was not difficult to find, as it was advertised on a billboard on the main road and was located at the edge of a small village, with a forest and a chain of green hills stretching out behind it. Set in its own grounds, it was very picturesque and clearly well cared for, with an outdoor swimming pool, landscaped gardens with fountains, flowerbeds and a golf course. It had that quiet, stately atmosphere that makes you slow down and feel you have all the time in the world.

Once in the large foyer, which made you think you were on a tropical island, I walked up to the reception desk. An attentive clerk asked me if he could help me.

"I want to check something," I said, suddenly feeling self conscious and awkward. I pulled out the photograph. "I would like to know if this woman was booked in to your hotel on the night of September sixth."

The man looked at the photograph, then at me, incredulously.

"Madam," he said, "there are three hundred guests every night in this hotel. They come and they go all the time." As he spoke, a bellboy appeared behind the desk and as he reached for the key to one of the rooms, he craned his neck, trying to catch a glimpse of the picture. The clerk looked at him admonishingly and handed me back the picture.

"I can't possibly remember," he said and added, "sorry," in a tone that sounded final and clearly marked the end of the conversation. I felt crestfallen and stood there for a moment, not knowing how to proceed further. The clerk then leaned over the counter and added in a hushed voice, "Unless this is part of an official investigation, we pride ourselves on our discretion. We do not disclose guests' details to anyone."

"I understand," I replied as I put the photograph away. "Thank you for your time," I said, turning away and feeling that it wasn't all right at all and that I had just wasted my time. I slowly walked to the door.

As I left the hotel and made my way toward the car, I saw a figure

The Discovery

approaching me from the side entrance to the hotel. It was the bellboy whom I had seen earlier behind the desk.

"I saw the picture," he said, as he approached me, "and I remember the girl," he added quickly, as if trying to hold my attention before I walked away. "She was here," he said firmly.

I opened my purse and pulled out a twenty-dollar bill.

"How can you remember?" I asked, handing him the banknote.

"I only remember because that was the day of my sister's wedding," he said, taking the money and putting it into his pocket with the speed of a true professional informer. "And I was due to be best man, so I was in a hurry to leave work. It was the end of my shift and I was really off duty, but those were the last guests that I was escorting to their rooms. You see, John, that's the guy who had the next shift after me, was late and I was filling in for him while he was getting changed into his uniform. I remember because we had an argument about it, but the manager asked me to stay on for half an hour longer, so I did. That lady—the one in the photograph—" he added, "was being very fussy, asking me questions about the place, about meal times, pool times, gym times, even though it's all written down in the brochure. Then she got me to shift the suitcase from the stand to the bed, checked out the bathroom, the closet and the tea service. I remember her because I was almost late for my sister's wedding."

"You have an extraordinary memory," I said while thinking that it sounded just like Anne—fussy and very particular. She was, after all, a Virgo. I was convinced it had to have been her. Once again I pulled the photograph out of my purse and handed it to the bellboy.

"Are you quite sure?" I asked.

"Yes ma'am, I am certain," the boy said. "I hope that will be all. I've got to go now. I'm still on duty." He brought his two fingers up to his cap in a kind of salute, pivoted on his toe and began walking back to the entrance of the hotel.

I was left there, standing in the middle of the driveway, still holding that photograph from a year ago. So it is her, was all that kept reverberating through my head. It's her. Suddenly, in my mind Anne was the villain, the false friend, the husband stealer, cold and destructive, cruel and uncaring—the vamp, the *femme fatale*, the family breaker.

www.ingramcontent.com/pod-product-compliance
Lightning Source LLC
Chambersburg PA
CBHW020928090426
42736CB00010B/1076